Christianity and Racism

Christianity and Racism

by

Bob Hellmann

Christianity and Racism
ISBN 0-927936-71-2
Copyright © 1995 by
Bob Hellmann
P. O. Drawer 17529
Huntsville, AL 35810

Published by
VINCOM, Inc.
P. O. Box 702400
Tulsa, OK 74170
(918) 254-1276

Dedication

To my wife Glo, from whose lips I have never heard a discouraging word.

To all the wonderful people who comprise Word of Truth World Outreach Church.

To my Lord Jesus, Who for whatever reason, has chosen me to help tear down racial barriers among His people.

Contents

Foreword

By Carlton Pearson

The New Testament Church, an inner-city fellowship, set the example for generations of churchgoers to follow. Diversity was the watchword. Jesus had come to bring unity among all people, and the Church was to be a reflection of the unconditional love of Christ.

Unfortunately, differences soon divided divine direction. For centuries, class, culture and color have created congregations content with exclusive fellowship. Racism barriers have been as prevalent in the Church as in society.

In 1906 when God began to pour out His Spirit at Azusa Street, unity surfaced. However, human nature again hindered God's perfect will for His Body. Believers failed to answer the call to wholeness. The Body of Christ was in pieces, disunited, disjointed, and the move of the Spirit was disrupted by disharmony.

Now, almost ninety years later, we still are struggling with divisive issues, and time is running out. If we want the full blessing of God, if we want to be a loud voice of healing to a dying, hurting world, then we must come together.

For years I have stated my heart's desire for unity in the Body. I have believed that as we come together in worship, we are like a stew. We have been likened to a melting pot, but that has been unrealistic. In a melting pot, the ingredients lose their uniqueness, and all blend into a mush that is unrecognizable. In a stew, however, the vegetables and meat retain their own special shape and color. In the cooking process, we stay unique, yet take on the same flavor.

Bob Hellmann addresses in great detail many of the issues we have taken with one another. You will find some specific healing points as this word takes aim at your fear and prejudice.

This book will challenge you to change your thinking. You will receive understanding and truth to live by as well as to share with others in the Body.

Introduction

Prejudice and racism have existed in the Church of the living God almost from the beginning of its inception. In the book of Acts, the early church suffered many such blows between the first disciples, the Jews and the Gentiles. The problem proved to be so great that God Himself addressed the issue by giving the Apostle Peter a tremendous vision of every unclean animal being set before him as potential food. (Acts 10:13,14 KJV.) The scripture professes that God said, **Rise, Peter; kill, and eat**, to which Peter religiously responded, **Not so, Lord; for I have never eaten any thing that is common or unclean**.

Much of the Church of Jesus Christ still suffers this extraordinary malady, thinking that the way they have learned supersedes the ways and the will of God Almighty! Peter, in his eagerness to live according to his own standard, neglected to realize that anything God sanctified was clean for his use.

Likewise, it's time for the Body of Christ to realize that God made provision for all people to enter into His covenant, and no one is to be denied. This was the lesson Jesus so appropriately and emphatically taught Peter on that fateful day. Immediately, Peter received a mighty deliverance from his prejudice. Along with it, God provided an opportunity for him to prove that he not only received it but was capable of walking in it.

Cornelius' household dramatically changed that day because the Lord Jesus Christ addressed Peter's not so unique prejudice. Ultimately, the Kingdom of God was openly preached to the Gentiles. God has been so addressing racism in His house since that day.

The Civil Rights Movement of the 60s and 70s actually started as a legitimate move of God upon an extremely racist nation. Its progenitors found its fathers actively involved in the call to ministry in its earliest roots. However, as soon as the movement came out of the house of God and into the political arena, its fate was sealed. The will of God will never be done if taken away from His concepts. Therefore, the Civil Rights Movement, as a political entity, cannot successfully destroy the ancient roots of racism.

Racism is a spirit, and it must be addressed through the power of the Spirit, God's Spirit. The Azusa Street Revival at the turn of the century marked a major attempt to address the issues of racism in the American church. The church failed then, as it did with the later Civil Rights Movement. She must not fail now!

Through this book, *Christianity and Racism*, author Bob Hellmann expresses proof of having had a visitation from Almighty God concerning racism and the Church. Just as with Peter, God has done an extraordinary feat in having a caucasian pastor, pastoring in the deep, prejudiced southern part of America, write a book concerning the evils of racism. Much of the Church world would rather take the posture of sticking its head in the sand as an ostrich, rather than face the fact that this evil has continued to permeate the best and most sanctified of churches.

Unless an ax is finally laid to the root of this tree, we will see the demise of the strength of God's house, coupled with trials as we have never experienced before. **Be not deceived; God is not mocked...** (Galatians 6:7a KJV). It is up to us in this generation, as the Church, to hear the alarm that is being sounded in these pages and respond with obedience, forgiveness, acceptance and love, allowing God to inundate us with a deep, rich healing. Unity and demonstration of Jesus' greatness will be the result.

Within these pages, each of us will find an exploration of the black culture from a biblical perspective. We will see how black/white racism began in America and God's answer as to how to end it. There is practical wisdom concerning how to entreat people of other cultures (more specifically, blacks), causing all people to be treated with the same grace and dignity that God treats them. This work testifies of the power of God to create brotherhood between the races, and the exemplary accomplishment of a multicutural, multi-racial church deeply rooted in His love.

The Word of God says, **Except the Lord build the house, they labour in vain that build it...** (Psalm 127:1a KJV). This house, called the building of God, must complete its metamorphosis as an entity that functions in the power of love and commitment. We must, as the Church, destroy every lasting bastian of slavery, realizing there is nothing wrong with being different, it is only wrong to divide because of racial differences.

God's creation is wondrously beautiful. Writing this book is a triumph in itself for the author and the people of God. Pastor Hellmann is to be commended for his diligence and boldness for producing such a timely work.

As you read this provocative book, allow its cleansing ability to prepare you for the "greatest move of God" in the history of the Church. If we allow this reconstructing piece to work in our lives, finally we will fulfill the scripture that says, **There is neither Greek nor Jew, circumcision nor uncircumcision, Barbarian, Scythian, bond nor free: but Christ is all, and in all** (Colossians 3:11 KJV).

Pam Vinnett

1

A Prophetic Forecast

One of the most enlightening books about American racism explains why racial disparities still persist in our twentieth century. In his book, **Two Nations, Black and White, Separate, Hostile, Unequal**, Andrew Hacker presents startling statistics which clearly show the gap in the critically drawn color lines. He offers bleak expectations for the future, "Only those willing to adapt to white expectations will succeed."

The Pulitzer prize-winning author, Arthur M. Schesinger, Jr., sends a warning in his book, **The Disuniting of America, Reflections on a Multicultural Society**. He states that the long-overdue recognition of the achievements of women, black Americans, Indians, Latinos and Asians has its price. If it is pressed too far, it poises this danger: the fragmentation, resegregation and tribalization of American life.

These are the words and forecasts of the secularists. While their words may be true about society as a whole, they do not know that God is doing something great in the land, especially in the Church.

Yes, the wind of God is blowing again across the land. You can see it in the many new movements now taking place. When God breathes His Spirit upon His Church, things change. They must. All living things must change or die. In fact, only dead things don't

1

change. A person enters a cycle of regression the instant he refuses to change.

The Spirit of God is doing something new and exciting among men. Racial barriers are coming down by the Spirit of God. Just as Communism crashed and the Berlin wall came down, racism is crumbling. Racial strongholds are falling in the house of the Lord.

God brought social reformation in the 1960s, but what is happening now is much deeper than that. This is a spiritual reformation that is now taking place. The 60s brought a change of law; the 90s will bring a change of heart. The reformation of the 60s was led by a man, but the reformation of the 90s is being led by the Spirit Himself. God is determined to bring blacks and whites together as one in His Son, Jesus Christ. It is beginning to happen now, but will escalate greatly in the days ahead.

As with all moves of God, there will be those who are pioneers in this movement and they will be the ones to pay the price. Not everyone wants black and white to come together. Even those in the house of God may fight and resist the change.

Black brothers and sisters who refuse to walk in bitterness, unforgiveness and resentment will be put to the test by family and a segment of the black citizenry. They will be called "Oreos," "Uncle Toms" and other such names. Great pressure will be brought by some of the black churches and intellectual community to make you feel like a modern-day traitor. You will be hailed as one who is leaving "your people" and "your culture." You will be seen as one who is betraying "the cause." It will be said that you are becoming white.

Bitterness and hatred have long arms, and they will not want to let you go. All who refuse to stay enlisted in the army of hate will be persecuted. This is true for white brothers and sisters also. White brothers and sisters will be severely tested. The secret and hidden places in a man will be judged during this time. Thoughts, motives and attitudes, which have been buried and concealed for a lifetime, will be confronted by the Spirit and brought to light. The subject of race cuts deep into the human heart and soul. In fact, nothing cuts so deeply into a man as racial truth.

It has long been known that if you really want to see a person's heart, look at what he does with his money, for where your treasure is there will your heart be also. (Matt. 6:21.) But racial issues cut into a person even deeper than money.

Get ready! God is bringing the races together in the house of the Lord. As this move of God gains strength, every prejudiced bone in your body will be confronted. When that happens, stand still and let God work in you. Don't run away. Don't try to avoid the dealings of God. Submit to Him and yield yourself to His work *in you*. Be honest. Stop lying to yourself. Don't deny that there are things in your heart that should not be there. Allow the Holy Spirit to create a clean heart within you.

This move of the Spirit, to break down racial barriers and strongholds, will be a move of great purity and holiness because the Spirit is going to reveal the ill will that has been hidden in our hearts. When our innermost secret attitudes of prejudice and hostility have been exposed, we can be set free. But it will not be pleasant for those who deny their prejudice and refuse to repent. You may put on a "Christian face" and say you're not prejudiced, but that will not suffice with the living God who sees and knows the heart! As God moves over His people by His Spirit, be assured that He is going to dig deep to get prejudice out of the heart of all who call on His name.

As God brings black and white together, don't be surprised at the attitudes and thoughts that surface within. Society has had many years to plant its poisonous seeds of prejudice in your mind. Now is the time to confess, repent and become clean before God. God desires truth in the inward parts, and there is no fooling Him.

Don't be self-deceived. Face the fact that you are prejudiced. Lay the ax at the root of that poisonous tree in your life and cut it down. It is better to judge yourself than to fall under judgment. (1 Cor. 11:31.)

Those who flow with this work of the Spirit and eagerly open the doors of their hearts to the unbiased love of God, are going to please God and experience a great joy and approval from the Lord.

But I caution you, don't run out of your church when God begins to do this work of bringing people of different races together. You are not being "led" to another church. You are prejudiced and you are using all kinds of excuses to get away. God knows the truth! And God knows you! Black people or white people coming into the church is not the real problem. Your sinful heart is the problem. The presence of black people or white people has triggered a negative, evil reaction within you. That evil reaction is called *prejudice*. Another name for it is sin! A person of another color is not the problem. The reaction of the heart is the problem.

As with every move of God, there will be those who rebel against what God is doing. Many will harden their hearts. Whole churches will publish statements of hate and segregation. They will even use the Bible. But remember, even Satan knows how to use, or should I say misuse, the Bible.

More and more, churches across the land will be multiracial, multicultured and multicolored. The all-white or all-black churches will exist only as dinosaurs of the past, facing extinction as they refuse to adapt to the new environment and social harmony of the true Church of the living God.

This move of God is not going to make all of us alike. We are diverse and we're not supposed to be clones of one another. It is going to bring all of us together in true love and unity and make us like Jesus. The goal of the white man is not to be like the black man, and the goal of the black man is not to be like the white man. No, our goal is to be like Jesus.

Make a commitment to walk in love. Your priority and calling is to be Christian, not black; to be Christian, not white.

Stop excusing your prejudice and quit blaming others. Stop living in the past. Today is a new day. Make an honest attempt to understand and appreciate people who are different. Deal with all the prejudicial thoughts that have been sown in your mind. These are weeds that must be pulled. Let God fill you with His love. His love is unconditional, unmerited and unmarked by prejudice of any kind.

Have an open mind. Realize that everything you heard or learned as a child was not right. Many things were said to you about black people or white people that were not true. Let God show you the beautiful qualities of people.

God is changing the hearts of men. Prepare your heart to learn. Prepare yourself for positive, godly

change. You are on the brink of some of the most exciting times in the history of mankind.

Don't be left behind. As you read, allow the Holy
Spirit to change your thinking. Renew your mind with
the Word of God. Let the truth of Christ come alive in
your heart.

2
Natural History and Supernatural History

Most people are so blinded to the truth of God when it comes to understanding the workings of God among the nations and races of men. God surely sees things differently than we do. He also has put certain spiritual laws into motion that govern the affairs of men. These spiritual laws are as real and certain as the natural laws that govern our universe. If we are ignorant of these spiritual laws, or if we are blinded to them, we will not understand the real causes for the things that happen to mankind. Therefore, instead of seeing sin as the real culprit on the earth, we will be busy blaming and fighting one another.

This chapter is about having the mind of God. What was God's purpose for the Revolutionary War and Civil War? Why were the lands of the Native Americans taken away from them and given to another nation? Why were the African people of the 1600s and 1700s enslaved? Why did God allow the atomic bomb to be dropped on Japan in World War II? Why did God not stop Hitler from killing six million Jews?

These are tough questions, but the answers are in the Word of God. The real answers for the things that happen to man are spiritual.

People have their own perceptions of the things that have happened over the last 350 years. Often, our perceptions are not correct. We need the mind of God, not the mind of the lost, carnal man. We need to see things the way God sees them.

Let us be on guard against the thinking that our natural, earthly point of view is the correct one. Pride will keep our hearts and minds closed to spiritual truth and cause us to remain in the bondage of bitterness and ill will. Being certain that we are right is a wrong approach to understanding the past. We are children of God, not children of this world. We should therefore see things spiritually, not carnally.

We need an enormous mental transformation in our understanding of the races. We need to be delivered from thoughts, ideas, concepts and philosophies that are of this world and not of the Lord Jesus Christ. We need to be delivered from our biased viewpoints so that we can acknowledge the truth of God.

Perception is important. Perception is how we see, understand and interpret the things that have happened to us.

Prior to "The Enlightenment" of the 1700s, man tended to see and interpret everything spiritually. The Enlightenment changed man's perceptions of himself and the world, from a sacred and spiritual understanding to a non-religious, secular one. During this time, man rejected God and committed himself to secular views based on reason or human understanding only. This intellectual movement advocated a philosophical rationalism deriving its methods from science and natural philosophy and replaced religion as the means of knowing nature and the destiny of humanity.

The great thinkers and philosophers of the Enlightenment were materialists, pantheists or atheists. The stories of Benjamin Franklin, the widely imitated essays of Joseph Addison and Richard Steele, and many dictionaries, handbooks and encyclopedias produced by the "enlightened" were written to popularize, simplify and promote a more "reasonable" view of life among the people of their time.[1]

In short, spiritual perception and interpretation were rejected, and what was reasonable to the mind and intellect of man was accepted.

The atheistic philosophies of the Enlightenment continue to this day, being touted in every high school and university in the land. That is the very reason society clashes with the mind of God as revealed in the Bible. No wonder our interpretation of wars and human events is secular.

In Luke, the Lord Jesus said, **How is it you don't know how to interpret this present time?** (Luke 12:56). Most of us do not know how to spiritually interpret the events that are happening before our very eyes or how to spiritually interpret the events of the past. When looking at the history of man, we tend to see things from the natural, human point of view. Paul said, **Do I say this merely from a human point of view?** (1 Cor. 9:8). There is a natural, human perspective of everything.

We are well aware of the different human points of view in regard to most subjects. We were all taught to see history from a natural, secular viewpoint. We do not have any kind of spiritual comprehension of world events. If we do not understand God's dealings with man and learn the principles of God from our study of the Word of God, then we are stuck with a shallow, earthly understanding.

According to Scripture, there is also a worldly point of view. Paul says, **So from now on we regard no one from a worldly point of view** (2 Cor. 5:16). Worldly people teach a carnal, secular, unspiritual philosophy and outlook. Most of us have been recipients of the world's educational system. From that system we received a secular view of history, science, philosophy, psychology and most other subject matters. Lost, worldly people put carnal concepts, ideas and interpretations into our minds. We carry these thoughts with us throughout our lifetime. Therefore, our understanding of most things is carnal. No wonder the Bible says that as Christians we must be changed by the renewing of our mind. Let us not conform to the natural ideas, philosophies and interpretations of this lost world. Be transformed by the Word of God. (Rom. 12:2.)

The word *repent* means to think differently, to have a change of mind.[2] After salvation we have a lot of "unlearning" to do. There are many things we need to change our mind about. True salvation causes one to see things differently. If you do not go through this process of unlearning worldly, carnal philosophies, you are going to be inhibited in your walk with the Lord and in your understanding of the world around you. You may have come out of Egypt, but God must now get Egypt out of you. If you are a graduate of the "University of Egypt," you are going to have a hard time with the way God thinks.

A classic example of the clashing of viewpoints is the debate concerning creationism and evolution. Evolution developed during the Enlightenment and is the worldly perspective of how we all got here. Creationism is the spiritual perspective. When Jesus comes to live in your heart, He is going to change your mind about many things, because you will begin to have a spiritual perspective. The Word of God will change the way you see. It will change your understanding and give you a different point of view. We must take off our secular glasses and have our true vision restored.

There is a secular side to life and a spiritual side to life. Secular people see the natural. Spiritual people see with eternal perspective. I do not mean to imply that life is either all secular or all spiritual. There should be a balance.

It is the clear teaching of Scripture that all who are spiritually lost are blinded to God's truth. They cannot see, understand or comprehend spiritual truth. They are totally ignorant of the Word of God. **The man without the Spirit does not accept the things that come from the Spirit of God, for they are foolishness to him, and he cannot understand them, because they are spiritually discerned** (1 Cor. 2:14).

When it comes to evolution, the differences of views on that particular subject are well known, but when interpreting history, we don't have two perspectives. All we have is the secular viewpoint. How could spiritually blinded instructors and professors give you anything but their worldly view? When a lost white professor or a lost black professor stands before the class and teaches on the races, slavery and prejudice, you are not going to get the mind of God on the subject!

An example of differing viewpoints is the change in our thinking of Columbus' discovery of America. Years ago Christopher Columbus was a hero. Today he is despised by those with a worldly, "enlightened" point of view, because his discovery led to the near extinction of the American Indian or Native American. Those who teach about Columbus today are teaching from a rational viewpoint, not a heavenly one.

Biblically speaking, there are deep spiritual reasons for the things that take place among the nations. For example, the Bible teaches that the real cause of drought is sin. Drought, therefore, is a spiritual problem, not a scientific one. Having a spiritual perception such as this is considered by the scientific community as reverting back into the dark ages. They do not believe the Word of God which clearly states, **So if you faithfully obey the commands I am giving you today — to love the Lord your God and to serve him with all your heart and with all your soul — then I will send rain on your land** (Deut. 11:13,14). **When the heavens are shut up and there is no rain because your people have sinned** (1 Kings 8:35). **When I shut up the heavens so that there is no rain...if my people, who are called by my name, will humble themselves and pray and seek my face and turn from their wicked ways, then will I hear from heaven and will forgive their sin and will heal their land** (2 Chron. 7:13,14).

God knows more than the scientist. True science does not contradict spiritual laws, it corroborates them. The Bible reveals that there is a knowledge that is falsely called science. All atheistic science is a false science. (1 Tim. 6:20 KJV.)

As in the case of a drought, we typically look only on the surface of things. (2 Cor. 10:7.) We are armed with our scientific reasoning for the events that take place on the earth. There are, however, deeper spiritual causes for the things that happen. Most people only relate to the rational point of view when it comes to understanding the things that happen on planet earth.

Because people look only on the surface of things, and because the world judges by human standards (John 8:15) and not God's, they do not have God's truth. There is a Biblical, scriptural point of view to everything. If only we had the mind of Christ and could see things as He does. God says, **"For my thoughts are not your thoughts, neither are your ways my ways," declares the Lord. "As the heavens are higher than the earth, so are my ways higher than your ways and my thoughts than your thoughts"** (Isa. 55:8,9). God's perspective is higher than our natural point of view. We need spiritual vision and understanding. The only way to get God's perspective is through the Holy Spirit and by reading the Word of God again and again.

This is why people of the world and people of the Word see things so differently. There are great philosophical clashes taking place in society today. These clashes are between the saved and the lost. One has the mind of God, the other has the mind of this world. One sees things spiritually, the other sees things secularly.

Abortion would be another example of a great philosophical war now taking place in our nation. There are only two views. The "enlightened," secular view — pro-choice, and the Biblical, sacred view — pro-life. Worldly people believe in abortion. Spiritual people don't. People from the "University of Egypt" believe in abortion. People of the Holy Scriptures don't. People with the mind of the world want abortion. People with the mind of God don't. This is a classic example of a battle that we could name, "The Enlightenment vs. The Word of God."

For man to get a correct view of things, he must go higher than the knowledge offered by the world.

My city is located in a valley. In fact, we call it the Tennessee Valley. While in the city, all you can see is what is directly in front of you and around you. From where I am in the city, I cannot see other sections of town. If you want to see the whole city, then go up on the mountain. While up high, you can see things that ordinarily you would not see.

That's the way we are with understanding human events. Because we are right down in the middle of it, "we can't see the forest for the trees." But God is not in the middle of it. He is high and lifted up and His throne is in heaven. He sees things from a heavenly perspective and not an earthly one. Since we are His children and have His Word and His Spirit, we should see things from His point of view and not from hearts that have been filled with secular concepts.

Since all the treasures of wisdom and knowledge are in Christ, we have to climb higher than the natural man to see the truth. God is the God of eternity. That is what is meant by the statement that Jesus is the Alpha and Omega. (Rev. 21:6.) He existed before the beginning of history, and He will be present at the end. Only God knows the real truth concerning the affairs of men and nations. He has shared many of these truths with us in His Word.

Concerning our example of Christopher Columbus, God's perspective, or the spiritual perspective of the discovery of the America's, would be threefold:

1. God is sovereign and wanted the new world discovered at this particular time for His purposes.

2. God is a Judge, and He judges nations and peoples when their sin reaches a certain measure and climax. (Gen. 15:16.) He brought judgment on a people who were paganistic and steeped in idolatry.

This point needs some commentary. Knowing God as a God of judgment is not popular these days. The New Age Movement does not believe in a God of judgment. They believe in a lovie-dovie God. Their philosophy and literature have infiltrated even Christian circles. It is difficult to find Christian leaders who believe in and acknowledge that God is a God of judgment.

We all need to learn the lesson that Nebuchadnezzar learned. Nebuchadnezzar was the king of Babylon. God used him to bring judgment on the Israelites because the Israelites were practicing idolatry. While reigning as king, Nebuchadnezzar had dreams from God. One of his dreams was sent to teach him that God is sovereign over the peoples of this world. The Scripture reads, **So that the living may know that the Most High is sovereign over the kingdoms of men and gives them to anyone he wishes and sets over them the lowliest of men** (Dan. 4:17). Daniel said yet again, **Seven times will pass by for you until you acknowledge that the Most High is sovereign over the kingdoms of men and gives them to anyone he wishes...Your kingdom will be restored to you when you acknowledge that Heaven rules** (Dan. 4:25,26).

This is a divine truth that we best not forget, even in this day when rationalism and humanism reign. After God dealt with Nebuchadnezzar's pride, Nebuchadnezzar said, **Then I praised the Most High; I honored and glorified him who lives forever. His dominion is an eternal dominion; his kingdom endures from generation to generation. All the peoples of the earth are regarded as nothing. He does as he pleases with the powers of heaven *and the peoples of the earth*. No one can hold back his hand or say to him: "What have you done?"...Everything he does is right and all his ways are just** (Dan. 4:34,35,37).

People today sass God. I don't care what God does, it is right! God is God! Whatever He does is just, and we do not have the right to question Him. Victory lies in acknowledging our sins and the sins of our forefathers. Victory comes by submitting to God, not rebelling against Him.

Let's stop making everything a racial issue. God does not judge people because of their race. He judges them because of their sin. *Sin is the problem* in the earth, not skin!

If America continues her backsliding ways, the day may come when God will send a nation to subdue her. If that occurs, it won't happen because we are white, black, Asian or Native American. It will happen because we are sinners.

Interestingly enough, the Spirit of the Lord is moving in these very days to bless and heal Native Americans. Native Americans are God's creation, and Jesus died for them just like He did for everyone else. If you judge by secular rationalism, the only thing you see is white men being ruthless to Native Americans and running them off of their land. As you understand the principles of God and His sovereignty, you come to know that God judges idolatry and may use one nation to subdue another.

But judgment is over! We must reach out to Native Americans and embrace them with the love of Christ. Native Americans must repent and acknowledge the idolatrous past of their ancestors in order to move into the full blessing of God. However, this is where we can get off track.

Most Native Americans have never confessed that the worship of their forefathers was idolatrous and sinful. Without repentance and a knowledge of the truth, a pro-Native American tide will re-open our doors to the very idolatry that brought judgment in the first place.

Recently, the national news did a segment on a white buffalo that had been born in Wisconsin. The family who owns this buffalo calf is not Native American, but they said three to four thousand people come to see the calf every week. They leave gifts for the family and offerings for the calf. The Native American who was interviewed on this same program said that the birth of a white buffalo calf was comparable to the birth of Jesus Christ and according to legend was an omen of peace. He went on to say that it also was a sign that we were to treat Mother Earth with respect.

This is the very same kind of idolatry that brought judgment on Native Americans hundreds of years ago. Multitudes have not repented and accepted Christ! Beware of what is coming on America in the wake of this pro-Native American movement. Even Spirit-filled preachers and teachers are saying that white society owes Native Americans an apology. Not so! This has nothing to do with race. It has to do with sin!

How frightening to think that calf worship is alive in America. Israel worshipped a golden calf. Now people right here in America are worshipping a white one!

3. Columbus brought the truth of Christ into an area of the world where false religions and demonology had flourished.

Humanists cannot tolerate this interpretation of historical events. After all, they are atheist and interpret history rationally and atheistically. They interpret history and all subject matter as though there was not a God! When a humanist or secularist teaches the Civil War, they teach it as though God did not exist. When they teach science, they teach it as though there was no Creator. When approaching philosophy or psychology, they present it from the view that there is no God. But the Scripture says, **The fool says in his heart, "There is no God"** (Ps. 14:1).

As Christians, we must interpret history and human events in light of the truth that there is a God! We must interpret human events spiritually and not rationally. What is your understanding of historical events? Where did you get that understanding? Do you see human events from the natural, carnal point of view? Do you understand world events from a secular, rationalistic view? Do you have God's perspective on things?

Concerning racial topics, we know the natural perspectives of man. What is God's perspective? What is the spiritual point of view? Certainly God's truth will free us, heal us and cause us to love one another.

As we get started in our study of mankind and the races, I want to set before you the following eleven Biblical precepts:

1. God is the Creator of all men, races, and ethnic groups. **He himself gives all men life and breath and everything else. From one man he made every nation of men** (Acts 17:25,26).

2. God is no respecter of persons, races or nationalities. **I now realize how true it is that God does not show favoritism but accepts men from every nation who fear him and do what is right** (Acts 10:34,35).

3. God loves all men and all races. **For God so loved the world that he gave his one and only Son, that whoever believes in him shall not perish but have eternal life** (John 3:16).

4. Jesus Christ, the Son of God, died for all men, all races. He is the Savior of all men. **This is a trustworthy saying that deserves full acceptance...that we have put**

our hope in the living God, who is the Savior of all men, and especially of those who believe (1 Tim. 4:9,10).

5. No race, no ethnic group, no nationality is better than or superior to any other. Neither is one inferior to any other. **This righteousness from God comes through faith in Jesus Christ to all who believe. There is no difference** (Rom. 3:22).

6. All people are blood related and have their common ancestry and genealogy through Noah. **From one man** [Noah] **he made every nation of men** (Acts 17:26).

7. All men, all races and all ethnic groups have sinned and fallen short of the glory of God. **For all have sinned and fall short of the glory of God** (Rom. 3:23).

8. The Bible is the Word of God to all men. The Bible was not written by blond-haired, blue-eyed Caucasians. It is not the white man's Book. It is God's Book and belongs equally to all. **"Lord, who has believed our message?" Consequently, faith comes from hearing the message, and the message is heard through the word of Christ. But I ask: did they not hear? Of course they did: "Their voice has gone out into all the earth, their words to the ends of the world"** (Rom. 10:16-18).

9. Jesus Christ was not a blond-haired, blue-eyed Caucasian. He was a Jew, descended from Abraham. As such He was neither white nor black. **A record of the genealogy of Jesus Christ the son of David, the son of Abraham** (Matt. 1:1).

10. In Christ, there is neither black nor white, male nor female. We are all one in Him. **Here there is no Greek or Jew, circumcised or uncircumcised, barbarian, Scythian, slave or free, but Christ is all, and is in all** (Col. 3:11). **You are all sons of God through faith in Christ Jesus...There is neither Jew nor Greek, slave**

nor free, male nor female, for you are all one in Christ Jesus (Gal. 3:26,28).

11. All true Christians, no matter how diverse, are commanded by the Lord Jesus to love one another with the self-sacrificial love of God. **A new command I give you: Love one another. As I have loved you, so you must love one another. By this all men will know that you are my disciples, if you love one another** (John 13:34,35).

If God sees people, diverse people, all across this world, with eyes of love, compassion and equality, should we, who bear His name, not see one another as He does?

We must all be conformed into the loving image of Christ!

3

A Spiritual Perspective of Slavery

As one studies slavery, it is necessary to go to the source of truth. Many good books have been written on the subject, but there is only one Book of Truth and that is the Bible — the Word of God. Among other things, the Bible is a divinely inspired book of history. It is not a natural history written by the natural man with his slanted and oftentimes erroneous viewpoints. It is supernatural history — history told by God Himself as He sees it.

The Bible contains answers for the most puzzling problems of life, but whether we accept its answers is another story. If we reject the answers of the Word of God, the only thing left to do is to invent our own answers. Our man-made answers are not truth; they are concepts we have made up to appease ourselves.

Our thoughts and feelings about racial issues basically come out of our flesh. Instead of going to the Word of God for truthful answers, we are led by our own anger, bitterness and hatred. Thus, we stay in bondage because of a lack of Biblical truth. Knowing the truth is paramount. Jesus said, **If you hold to my teaching, you are really my disciples. Then you will know the truth, and the truth will set you free** (John 8:31,32). It is the teaching of Jesus Christ in the Word of God that sets people free in every area of life, including the area of racism.

It is important that we look at racial subjects spirit-ually rather than carnally. It is important that we look, even at the subject of slavery, from a spiritual per-spective instead of a worldly one. It is time we had the mind of God on racial matters instead of the mind of the natural man.

To know the truth about slavery, let's go to the Book — the Bible. The Word of God shows us that slavery is far from an American phenomenon. Slavery was not invented by the Caucasians of Europe or America. The white people of the seventeenth century were not the originators of slavery. Slavery started as soon as Noah and his family stepped off the ark into the new world.

The Bible tells the story of how it all came about. Ham, Noah's black son, greatly dishonored his father. In twentieth century America that doesn't mean much, but in that day and time and in that culture, it was a terrible sin. As a result of Ham's sin, Noah cursed one of Ham's black sons — Canaan. Noah said, **Cursed be Canaan! The lowest of slaves will he be to his brothers** (Gen. 9:25). With that pronouncement, slavery was born!

This is the very first time the word *slave* is used in the Bible, and the first time anyone became a slave. There are a number of truths for us to see here, so let's take a look at them one by one.

1. We clearly see that slavery is a curse. It is not a good thing. It is not a blessing.

2. The origin of slavery had nothing to do with skin color, race or geographic location. Thus, slavery was never a racial issue.

3. Canaan was not enslaved because he was infe-rior. He was enslaved because he was wicked. Slavery

was never an issue of superiority or inferiority. The Bible does not say that Canaan was inferior to other people.

4. Slavery was not an issue of intelligence. Every man of every race and color has been made in the image of God and possesses great intellectual potential.

5. The enslavement of Canaan came about because of *sin*. Sin brought enslavement into the human race. Sin, not skin, is the real problem in the earth. You will find this principle throughout the Bible and world history — slavery is one of the things that can happen to a people when they are in sin. Therefore, the Word of God shows slavery to be a spiritual issue, not a racial one!

For hundreds of years, lost people of this world have mistakenly taught the subject of slavery as a racial issue. But the Word of God clearly shows us that it is not a racial issue at all.

6. The reddish-brown Noah is the one who spoke the curse of slavery onto Canaan and into the human race. A white man did not initiate slavery.

7. Ham, the black son of Noah, was never cursed. Noah said, **Cursed be Canaan** (Gen. 9:25). He did not say, "Cursed be Ham." Furthermore, he did not say, "Cursed be Ham's seed."

8. Ham had four black sons in all: Cush, Mizraim, Put and Canaan. (Gen. 10:6.) When Noah spoke forth the curse of slavery, he spoke it only on Canaan! Cush, Mizraim and Put were not cursed or part of the curse of Noah!

This is extremely important because Cush, whose name literally means "of a black countenance,"[1] migrated to what is now called Africa and became the founder of Ethiopia. Thus, black Ethiopians were never cursed. They were never part of Noah's curse. Noah's curse did not affect Cush.

Mizraim, whose name literally means "Egypt,"[2] was obviously the founder of the great Egyptian people and kingdom. Mizraim was not cursed.

Put went to northern Africa and founded the nation of Libya. He was not cursed.

We see from this information that the curse of Noah did not affect any of the sons of Ham who settled in Africa. The black African people were never part of any curse!

Only Canaan was cursed, and he never settled in Africa. He migrated to that part of the world that is now occupied by Israel. In fact, much of the Old Testament is built around the truth that God called a man named Abraham and gave him the land of the Canaanite! God said to Abraham, **The whole land of Canaan, where you are now an alien, I will give as an everlasting possession to you and your descendants after you** (Gen. 17:8).

Because Satan has lied to black people so much and told them they are cursed, many blacks have turned to the nation of Islam instead of the Lord Jesus Christ. Satan has sold Christianity as the white man's religion, while Islam has been touted as the true religion of the black man.

African-Americans were made largely aware of the Islam faith through the efforts of an Omaha, Nebraska, native, Malcolm Little.

Convicted on burglary charges at the age of 21, Malcolm X, as he was later known, became a convert to the nation of Islam and a devout follower of Elijah

Muhammad while in prison. He dedicated only twelve years of his life to this branch of his faith, but in that time managed to win many converts with his strong emphasis on empowering the poor.[3]

The Islamic religion, based on the teaching of Muhammad, came into being in 610 A.D. when the "prophet" supposedly received a revelation through the angel Gabriel. Muhammad was a descendant of Ishmael, the son of Abraham and the Egyptian servant, Hagar.

Unrealized by many in the West, the majority of Muslims are not Arabs. Islam was born among the Arabs, but it has spread far beyond Arab lands. In fact, over three-fourths of the Islamic world lies outside the Arabic-speaking countries.

Today, there are over eight hundred million Muslims. Indonesia is the world's most populous Islamic nation with one hundred fifty million Muslims. Muslims in India number eighty-two million; in China, about forty million.

Even in the former Soviet Union, Islam is deeply entrenched. Daily newscasts show the fragmented nation's turmoil over the implications of shifting ethnic balances. By the year 2000, it is estimated every second child born in that region of the world will be of Muslim parentage.

Among the Islamic communities there is great division, even though they agree on almost all the basic essentials of their faith. About 85 percent are Sunnis. Fifteen percent are Shiites. Shiism, in turn, has split into an array of subsects and offshoots. The Ayatollah Khomeini was a Shiite.[4]

There is little in the colorful history of the Islamic faith that would suggest it is a black man's religion.

Wallace Fard was the first man to bring principles of the Islamic faith to American's shores in the early 1930s. Our nation was in the grip of the Great Depression. People were grasping at anything that would offer them a better life. The ideology of Communism in the United States saw a great rise at this time as well. Much about Wallace Fard remains a mystery. A study of his teachings reveals much of his doctrine was derived from the Koran. He also drew from books on Freemasonry, the Bible and the philosophies of Joseph F. Rutherford, a leader of the Jehovah's Witnesses.

Fard said he was born in Africa as a member of the Kuraish tribe — the same tribe as the founder of Islam, the "prophet" Muhammad. He went by several names including Wali Farrad, Professor Ford, Farrad Mohammed, and on occasion, Allah (god).

Fard's teachings varied significantly from those of traditional Islam, which promotes the brotherhood between people of all races. One of his early followers, Elijah Poole, later renamed Elijah Muhammad, joined the Nation of Islam in 1931. Elijah Poole later said of Fard, "I recognized him to be God in person and that is what he said he was...I recognized him to be the person the Bible predicted would come two thousand years after Jesus' death." Fighting broke out within the nation of Islam and their "god" mysteriously disappeared in June of 1934.[5]

Elijah Muhammad (Poole) picked up the torch adding his own concepts. They would soon be promoted for a short time by the soon-to-be assassinated Malcom X. Louis Farrakhan continues to carry the message today. Blacks need not be enslaved any longer by the misguided teachings of Wallace Fard and his successors.

The truth is, the black descendants of Ham, with the lone exception of Canaan, have never been cursed. In fact, they were supernaturally blessed by God and in covenant with God. Genesis 9:1 says, *Then God blessed Noah and his sons,* **saying to them, "Be fruitful and increase in number and fill the earth."** God blessed Noah and each of his three sons. Noah's sons were Shem, Ham and Japheth (Gen. 9:18.) If God blessed Noah's sons, as Scripture says He did, then God blessed Shem. God blessed Ham and God blessed Japheth. Noah's three sons were blessed. When Ham sinned, one reason Noah did not say, "Cursed be Ham," was because Ham was blessed of God. Man cannot curse what God has blessed! Thus, the curse went to Canaan.

Genesis 9:8 says, **Then God said to Noah and to his sons with him: "I now establish my covenant with you and with your descendants after you."** Noah, Shem, Ham and Japheth were each in covenant relationship with God. So we see that the black Ham was blessed of God and in covenant with God.

After the flood, the first great men on the earth were the black Hamites. They were extremely intelligent and ambitious. For a long period of time they controlled the earth and were the world's dominant race. They created the first great world kingdoms and empires, such as Assyria (Micah 5:6), Babylon, Nineveh, India and Egypt.

The black Hamites brought forth great inventions that are still with us today. Following is a list of inventions they contributed to civilization: pyramids, paper, mathematics, ceramics, running water, glass, food preservation, clocks, calendars, maps and iron-making.[6]

Modern black inventions include: dough kneader, mailbox, pencil sharpener, horseshoe, fountain pen, tricycle, golf tee, baby buggy, spark plug, almanac, dust pan, fire extinguisher, lawn sprinkler, lunch pail, rolling pen, ironing board, multi-barrel machine gun, folding chair, automatic gear shift, file folder, traffic light, gas mask, curtain rod supporter, curtains, lawn mower, blood plasma bag, egg beater, lemon squeezer, mop and telephone transmitter. Each of these items was created and patented by African-Americans. What a great list of accomplishments!

During the period of time when the black descendants of Ham were the dominant race on earth, they enslaved the olive-complected descendants of Shem and the white descendants of Japheth. The first king on the earth after the flood was Nimrod. Nimrod was a black descendant of Cush, and he is called in the Scriptures, **a mighty hunter before the Lord** (Gen. 10:9). The term *mighty hunter* in Hebrew can mean a hunter of animals or of men to enslave them.[7] The word *mighty* means powerful, warrior, tyrant, champion, giant or valiant man.[8] The black Nimrod had a kingdom, which in Hebrew means "dominion." Thus, we see that the black Hamites were dominant on the earth after the flood.

There was a time when the black descendants of Ham enslaved the olive-complected Israelites for four hundred years. The Israelites were enslaved, held against their will and forced to do hard labor. (Gen. 15:13.) As slaves, they built two cities for Pharaoh. Scripture says:

> So they put slave masters over them to oppress them with forced labor, and they built Pithom and Rameses as store cities for Pharaoh.
>
> They made their lives bitter with hard labor in brick and mortar and with all kinds of work in the fields; in all their hard labor the Egyptians used them ruthlessly.
>
> **Exodus 1:11,14**

Here is a clear picture of the black Hamites enslaving the olive-skinned Shemites. Don't think that Caucasians are the only race of people who have enslaved others. That is not true at all.

Over the last six thousand years, millions of people have known what it is like to be a slave of man. Among some black people, there is the thought that they are the only people who have been through the horrors and injustices of slavery. Not so!

After the Hamites, the descendants of Shem began to rise and became the governing race on earth almost until the time of Christ. They, too, enslaved people.

White people themselves have been enslaved. While Paul was in Macedonia, we are told the story of a slave girl who followed Paul around. This slave girl was probably white since Paul was in an area of the world inhabited by Japheth's Caucasian descendants. (Acts 16:16-18.)

There was a period of time (440 A.D.) when the Huns from Mongolia, under the leadership of Attila the Hun, raided Europe and enslaved white Roman and Germanic peoples.[9]

Leif Erickson, the famous Viking, is said to have had a young white German slave.

The point is, black people are not the only ones who have been enslaved. In fact, the descendants of Shem, Ham and Japheth have each been enslaved at one time or another.

We now live in the period of time when the descendants of Japheth are the controlling race on earth. Each race of men has had a turn in ruling the earth. Each race, while contributing both good and bad to the human condition, has basically made a mess of things.

Lost man, no matter what color, has not done a good job of running this planet. Since the Hamites, Shemites and Japhethites have all had their turn of ruling and reigning, the next to rule will be the Lord Jesus Christ!

What I want to focus on now is why people have been enslaved throughout world history. It is extremely important to see that, according to the Word of God, slavery is not a racial matter but a spiritual matter.

Our case study will be the Israelites themselves. After their enslavement in Egypt, the people of Israel returned to the land of Abraham, Isaac and Jacob and became a great nation. God entered into special covenant with them and gave them the Ten Commandments. He also gave them warning as to what would happen if they violated His law.

> You who were as numerous as the stars in the sky will be left but few in number, *because you did not obey the Lord your God.*
>
> You will be uprooted from the land you are entering to possess.
>
> Then the Lord will scatter you among all nations.
>
> Deuteronomy 28:62-64

Israel did not obey God or heed His warning. Later in their history, they became terrible idolaters. It was their idolatry that caused them to be enslaved. Listen to what God says to Israel in Jeremiah.

> "You have rejected me," declares the Lord. "You keep on backsliding. So I will lay hands on you and destroy you.
>
> "I will bring bereavement and destruction on my people, for they have not changed their ways.
>
> "Your wealth and your treasures I will give as plunder, without charge, *because of all your sins throughout your country.*

> "I will enslave you to your enemies in a land
> you do not know, for my anger will kindle a fire that
> will burn against you."
>
> Jeremiah 15:6,7,13,14

Sin is what brings curses and slavery on men, races
and nations. The Bible is clear on the matter. If you
really want to see this principle, study Jeremiah and
Ezekiel and pay special attention to the word because.

Let's begin with Jeremiah 1:16. God says, **I will
pronounce my judgments on my people** *because of
their wickedness* **in forsaking me.** Jeremiah 3:21 continues, **A cry is heard on the barren heights, the
weeping and pleading of the people of Israel,** *because
they have perverted their ways and have forgotten the
Lord their God.*

Ezekiel says:

> **Son of man, when the people of Israel were
> living in their own land, they defiled it by their
> conduct and their actions.**
>
> **So I poured out my wrath on them** *because they
> had shed blood in the land and because they had defiled
> it with their idols.*
>
> **I dispersed them among the nations, and they
> were scattered through the countries; I judged them
> according to their conduct and their actions.**
>
> Ezekiel 36:17-19

Bad things were not happening to these people
because they were Jews. The racial way of looking at
this would be to bemoan the fact that they were Jews
and were therefore being mistreated and getting an
unfair deal in life. But the Bible makes it plain that it
was their forsaking the Lord that brought all of this on
them.

Judgments don't come on skin but on sin. When
something catastrophic happens to a nation or a people,

the root or the cause is spiritual, not natural. The root or the cause of everything that has happened to Israel is spiritual in nature. For example, when Jesus described the coming desolation of Jerusalem, He said, **They will dash you to the ground, you and the children within your walls. They will not leave one stone on another, because you did not recognize the time of God's coming to you** (Luke 19:44).

In 70 A.D., Titus destroyed Jerusalem just as Jesus had prophesied. But Titus did not destroy Jerusalem because the people there were Jews. It was their rejection of Jesus Christ as Messiah that caused this devastation and loss of life. Again, understand, there are spiritual reasons for the catastrophic things that happen to races and nations.

In fact, any people who forsake the true and living God are going to bring curses on themselves. That holds true for white people, black people, Native Americans, Asians, Europeans and all the people of the world.

With this Biblical foundation in place, let's turn our attention to modern times and the plight of the African 500 years ago. African slavery actually began as a black-on-black crime. African masters bought and sold slaves to extend their holdings. The first slaves shipped from Africa were sold by Africans in the 1400s to Spain. By 1500 Seville, Spain, had developed into a principal trading center for African slaves to the Americas.[10]

The very first Africans to arrive in America did not come as slaves but came soon after Columbus' first voyage, traveling as sailors, soldiers and workers. They helped to conquer the land and subdue the native American Indians.

Why were Africans enslaved hundreds of years ago? Was it because they were black? No! Was it because they were cursed by Noah? No! Were they inferior to other human beings? No! Could it be because they were involved in idolatry, witchcraft and spiritism? Yes! Sin, not skin, brings bad things on people. God basically did to Africans what He did to the people of Israel. Because of sin, more specifically the sin of idolatry, He uprooted them from their land and took them to a foreign country. But the real motive and heart of God was not to hurt the African people for whom Christ died, but to save them from their sin and bring them to Himself.

Judgment and slavery have not just happened to Africans. When Attila the Hun attacked Europe and enslaved white Roman and Germanic peoples, he was called "the Scourge of God." The white Romans were in idolatry, too. Caesar was regarded as a god and was called lord, so the sovereign God of heaven sent the pagan Attila to bring judgment on white European idolaters.

Just recently, archeologists have uncovered some ancient graves in England. Their findings show that many of the dead were sacrificed. Thus, Africa has by no means cornered the market on idolatry. Wherever a people have been idolatrous, God has always — sooner or later — brought them to judgment. Judgment comes on white idolaters, black idolaters, red idolaters, Asian idolaters and American idolaters. Sin and slavery are no respecter of persons. Neither is judgment.

The humanists of today criticize the United States for dropping the atomic bomb on the Japanese Empire at the end of World War II. These "enlightened rationalists" have turned the Japanese into the victims, while making America the violent aggressor. Their viewpoint is totally incorrect. They have things completely backwards. Furthermore, they have no spiritual knowledge or comprehension about the dropping of the atomic bomb.

What I am about to say is going to be very offensive to those who have graduated from the "University of the World," and hold a degree in secular humanism. The atomic bomb was actually a judgment from God on an extremely idolatrous people. The loss of life was tragic. Judgment of any kind is tragic. It is the last thing God resorts to when trying to get a nation's attention. God loves people — all people. He wants to save people. But when He has been spurned and rejected time and time again, there is nothing else to resort to but judgment. That is clearly the principle of the Word of God.

Speaking of Israel, Scripture says, **They did not obey you or follow your law; they did not do what you commanded them to do. So you brought all this disaster upon them** (Jer. 32:23). Jeremiah 40:2,3 says, **The Lord your God decreed this disaster for this place. And now the Lord has brought it about; he has done just as he said he would. All this happened because you people sinned against the Lord and did not obey him.**

Some may wonder, "What do these Scriptures about Israel have to do with other nations and peoples?" The answer is, God is the God of every nation, race and ethnic group. He is not just the God of Israel. He is the true God of Japan, Britain, Ethiopia, Egypt, Saudi Arabia, Peru, Mexico, America, China, Iran and every other country. The whole world is the Lord's and everything in it. (Ps. 24:1.) Every nation belongs to God. He expects every nation and race to worship Him. He is the one and only true and living God! Besides Him there is no other. Speaking of the name of Jesus, the Bible declares, **Salvation is found in no one else, for there is no other name under heaven given to men by which we must be saved** (Acts 4:12).

When any nation or people reject the God and Father of our Lord Jesus Christ, they are setting themselves up for judgment. Again, judgment comes only because of sin.

Getting back to the judgment of slavery, let's shift the focus of our attention now from the enslaved to the enslaver. In Israel's case, God used an ungodly king and an ungodly nation to bring judgment on Israel. Nebuchadnezzar was the king and Babylon was the nation. God says, **I will hand all Judah over to the king of Babylon, who will carry them away to Babylon or put them to the sword** (Jer. 20:4). Scriptures like these, and there are many of them especially in the Old Testament, show us that God is sovereign. He does whatever pleases Him, in the heavens and on the earth. (Ps.135:6.) Because God is sovereign He can use even the wicked to accomplish His purposes if He chooses to do so.

Nebuchadnezzar was an ungodly idolater himself. God did not use him because he was righteous or because he was better than the people of Israel. Here is a principle worth noting, God will use a wicked person, king or nation to bring judgment on another people or nation. Then, in His timing, He will punish the ungodly aggressor for their own wickedness. This is exactly what He did with Nebuchadnezzar and Babylon. God said, **"But when the seventy years are fulfilled, I will punish the king of Babylon and his nation, the land of the Babylonians, for their guilt,"** declares the Lord, **"and will make it desolate forever"** (Jer. 25:12).

Attila the Hun was a pagan, but the sovereign God of heaven used him, and as I said earlier, he was called "The Scourge of God."

Like Nebuchadnezzar, the white slave traders of the seventeenth and eighteenth centuries were wicked, evil men. They certainly did not go to Africa for the cause of Christ or for righteous reasons. In fact, the New Testament makes it plain that slave trading was a terrible sin and was contrary to the Gospel of Jesus Christ. Scripture says:

> **We also know that law is made not for the righteous but for lawbreakers and rebels, the ungodly and sinful, the unholy and irreligious; for those who kill their fathers or mothers, for murderers,**
>
> **For adulterers and perverts, for slave traders and liars and perjurers — and for whatever else is contrary to the sound doctrine**
>
> **That conforms to the glorious gospel of the blessed God, which he intrusted to me.**
>
> **1 Timothy 1:9-11**

Slave trading is listed with the worst sins a human can commit. It keeps company with rebels, the ungodly, the sinful, the unholy, murderers, perverts and liars. It was a sin compared to killing your own mother and father. The Bible says that slave trading was contrary to sound doctrine and contrary to the glorious Gospel of Jesus Christ. Slave trading was not part of the Gospel. It was in opposition to the Gospel.

Jesus told us to go into all the world and preach the Gospel to every creature. He did not say to go and make slaves out of people. We are to go and heal, not afflict. We are to set people free, not bind them up.

Another similarity of the white slave traders to Nebuchadnezzar is that God judged them. Many people are not aware of that. In fact, God judged America for its role in enslaving the African people. God's judgment on this country for its crimes against the African people was the Civil War. War many times is a judgment of God. The Bible says so.

Isaiah 42:24,25 says:

> Who handed Jacob over to become loot, and Israel to the plunderers? Was it not the Lord, against whom we have sinned? For they would not follow his ways; they did not obey his law.

> So he poured out on them his burning anger, the violence of war. It enveloped them in flames, yet they did not understand; it consumed them, but they did not take it to heart.

This Scripture says that war is God's burning anger. With that in mind, consider the Civil War. In the Civil War, approximately 1,000,000 white people lost their lives! Compare that with wars of the twentieth century. In World War I, America lost 50,585 men.[11] In World War II, the American death toll was 292,000 men. We lost 23,300 in the Korean War and 58,000 in Vietnam. If you add up these figures, you will find that 1,000,000 died in the Civil War and 423,885 died in *all the other wars combined*! The Civil War was clearly a judgment of God poured out on this country. Through the Civil War, God judged the generation that was most oppressive to the black African people.

God uses Nebuchadnezzars, but Nebuchadnezzar's time under the hand of God is coming.

What we really see in the white enslavement of the African people is sinful man, enslaving sinful man. The black African of 350 years ago was not a worshipper of the Lord Jesus. He was a worshipper of idols and spirits. The white European and American slave traders were involved in idolatry, too. The Bible teaches that the love of money or greed is idolatry. (Col. 3:5.) The Bible also shows us that slave trading is part of this world's depraved Babylonian system. (Rev. 18:1-13.)

Something that greatly hurt the cause of Christ was that these white slave traders and owners confessed to being Christians. Some would take their slaves to church with them on Sunday and then beat them later in the day. Clearly, these people did not know what it meant to be born again and have the Spirit of Christ indwell them. They were Christian in name only and not in experience. If a "Christian" was beating me, working me ruthlessly, selling my children and quoting Scriptures to me to keep me in line, I don't think I would ever want to be a "Christian." This was a horrible misrepresentation of Jesus Christ, Who loves all equally and Who died for all.

Someone may be wondering, "If slave trading is such a bad sin, why did God give regulations in both the Old and New Testaments concerning the owning of slaves?" It appears that God tolerated slavery just as He tolerated polygamy. Why were men allowed to have multiple wives? From the beginning of time it was clear that polygamy was not God's design. There were certain things that were not the express will of God that He tolerated for a time. Then, at a certain point, God put an end to it. With the death of Jesus Christ, that which was imperfect, like slavery and polygamy, was destined to vanish under the power of His holy blood.

Yes, there are spiritual causes for the things that happen to men, races and nations. Don't look at things carnally. Look at things spiritually.

Jesus Christ loves all men, races and nations. He died for all. He died for the black people of Africa, the white people of Europe, the Asian peoples of China and Japan and everyone else in this world.

Everyone has a right to Jesus and the love and salvation that He alone offers. He is not a white Jesus or a black Jesus. He is the Jesus of the Bible, the Son of God!

4

A Redemptive View of the Past

To understand the deeper purpose of God, we should look at Joseph and his enslavement.

As a young man, Joseph had a dream. It was a very unusual dream, but it was a dream from God. It was a revelation of the purpose of God for his future. It was not a revelation of the plan of God; that is, it was not a revelation of how God's purpose was going to be fulfilled. Let's not get God's purposes confused with His plans. God may show you His purpose for your life, but not reveal the plan of how He is going to bring about the purpose. Such was the case with Joseph.

Here is Joseph's dream:

> Joseph had a dream, and when he told it to his brothers, they hated him all the more.
>
> He said to them, "Listen to this dream I had:
>
> "We were binding sheaves of grain out in the field when suddenly my sheaf arose and stood upright, while your sheaves gathered around mine and bowed down to it."
>
> Genesis 37:5-7

Joseph's brothers understood what the dream meant. They said to him, "Do you intend to reign over us? Will you actually rule us?" The dream was a prophetic forecast that Joseph was one day going to be exalted over his brothers, and his brothers were going to bow down and pay homage to him.

If I had been Joseph, I'm sure I would have laid awake at night thinking, "How is God going to do this?" In my wildest imagination, I would never have thought God's lofty purpose was going to be achieved through the avenue of rejection and slavery.

While in the field one day, the brothers saw Joseph coming and quickly devised a plot to do away with him and his dream. They threw him into a pit and sold him to a group of passing Ishmaelites for twenty shekels of silver.

Joseph left home a favorite son, but by the end of the day he was a common slave. He left home that fateful morning not knowing that he would never return. As he went out on an errand for his father, he was abruptly apprehended, abducted, captured, snatched. Joseph's life was interrupted. His freedom was stolen. His future darkened. In the prime of his youth, he was reduced to a slave.

The Ishmaelites took him to Egypt, where he was sold a second time to Potiphar. Much to his consternation, he found himself in a foreign land, far from his beloved father, Jacob. There he sat, rejected and betrayed by his own flesh and blood. He had been sold for money like a piece of merchandise. He was now owned by another human being. He is shackled like a prisoner or perhaps like a dog.

And he sent a man before them — Joseph, sold as a slave.

They bruised his feet with shackles, his neck was put in irons.

Psalm 105:17,18

Even in slavery God was with him, and everything he did prospered. Potiphar put him in charge of his whole household and entrusted to his care everything he owned. All was well until Potiphar's wife desired Joseph and lied to her husband about him. She said, **That Hebrew slave you brought us came to me to make sport of me** (Gen. 39:17). She called him a slave because that is what he was. As a result of her falsehood, Joseph was soon put in prison. Now he is twice incarcerated — incarcerated as a slave and incarcerated in prison. Slavery is itself a prison, but God was with him.

Thirteen years pass and Joseph spends those years as a common slave with irons around his ankles and neck. One day God reached down and raised Joseph up and put him over the whole land of Egypt. Through the wisdom of God, Joseph devises a plan to save the whole land of Egypt during seven years of famine. Through Joseph, Egypt had plenty to eat while the rest of the Middle Eastern world was starving. Other nations start streaming to Egypt to get food. They all have to go through Joseph because he is the man in charge of food distribution. Who should show up one day for food but Joseph's brothers who sold him into slavery. They all bowed down to him in reverence and respect. Joseph's dream was fulfilled!

One day when the brothers came to Joseph, he decided to reveal his true identity to them. Genesis 45:3-5,7,8 tells the story. Here is what the Scripture says:

Joseph said to his brothers, "I am Joseph!

"I am your brother Joseph, the one you sold into Egypt!

"And now, do not be distressed and do not be angry with yourselves for selling me here, because it was *to save lives that God sent me ahead of you.*

"God sent me ahead of you to preserve for you a remnant on earth and to save your lives by a great deliverance.

"So then, it was not you who sent me here, but God!"

What an awesome statement! Joseph was not angry because of what had happened. He was not bitter. He was not fixing blame and plotting revenge. He was free from all of that. He was free because he saw the redemptive hand of God at work in his past, even in his slavery. He had a positive view of a negative past!

The black people of America can make the same kind of statement Joseph did. "It was to save lives that God sent my forefathers ahead of me. God sent them ahead of me to preserve for me a remnant on earth and to save our lives by a great deliverance. So then it was not man who put me here, but God!"

Does this absolve the white slave traders and owners? Absolutely not! Does this excuse white people who have been prejudiced for the last hundred years? No! Of course not! But it does help us see that the invisible hand of God was at work bringing good out of bad.

Joseph later said to his brothers, **You intended to harm me, but God intended it for good to accomplish what is now being done, the saving of many lives** (Gen. 50:20).

Men intend things for evil, but God intends things for good. God is a God Who saves! He does things in order to save people, not in order to harm them. This is in line with Psalm 68:20 which says, **Our God is a God who saves; from the Sovereign Lord comes escape**

from death. God is saving people even when it looks like He is not.

Who of us would rather be living in Africa today than right where we are? With the wars, famines, droughts and diseases, not to mention the ten million Africans who have AIDS, could God have intended the removal of the African people to America 350 years ago as a move to save future generations of a people He loved? Don't misunderstand me. Men, white men, intended slavery for evil, but we're not talking about men right now, we're talking about God! Don't you think it's time we got God's perspective on the situation? I know what the black viewpoint is. I know what the white viewpoint is. But what is the eternal purpose of God?

What is disturbing is that many people, black and white, hold to the natural, rational viewpoint of the world on this subject. The redeemed, born-again people of God should not have a worldly viewpoint of such matters, but a heavenly one. The Bible warns us, **See to it that no one takes you captive through hollow and deceptive philosophy, which depends on human tradition and the basic principles of this world rather than on Christ** (Col. 2:8).

Lost, worldly people, black and white, only know lost, worldly philosophy. They speak lost, worldly philosophy. They teach lost, worldly philosophy. They are not speaking the Word of God or the mind of Christ. We are all destroyed for lack of knowledge of God. Millions of white people and black people are this very hour held captive by false, deceptive philosophies of this lost world. It only takes one lie of the devil to ruin your whole life and hold you captive. One lie can keep you in negativism, bitterness or prejudice for fifty years.

Both white and black people are incarcerated by lies, perpetuated by lost people of both races.

Even some preachers preach racial mythology, prejudice and hate from the pulpit, all in the name of the Lord. Any preacher preaching hatred in the name of Jesus is a liar and charlatan. The Scriptures are plain. First John 3:10 says, **This is how we know who the children of God are and who the children of the devil are: Anyone who does not do what is right is not a child of God;** *nor is anyone who does not love his brother*. The Scriptures go on to say, **We know that we have passed from death to life, because we love our brothers. Anyone who does not love remains in death. Anyone who hates his brother is a murderer, and you know that no murderer has eternal life in him** (1 John 3:14,15).

Brother in Biblical language means Christian brother, not racial brother. The Bible that says **God is love** (1 John 4:16) is not going to teach you to hate anybody! Hate is of the devil, and all who preach hate are of the devil and are speaking his words, not God's! (John 8:44.) If you are in a church that is teaching you to hate anybody, get out of it immediately! Any such pastor, elder, apostle, bishop or preacher is as the following verses describe:

> **For such men are false apostles, deceitful workmen, masquerading as apostles of Christ.**
>
> **And no wonder, for Satan himself masquerades as an angel of light.**
>
> **It is not surprising, then, if his servants masquerade as servants of righteousness. Their end will be what their actions deserve.**
>
> **2 Corinthians 11:13-15**

We should get our eyes off of man and onto the Lord. God has judged the white slave traders and owners, and He will judge prejudice in the hearts of all, white and black. Let God be the Judge, but let us see the Lord and His purpose. How much better it would be for us to get our eyes off of the "way we got here" and "the color of the people who brought us here" and on to the truth that God was saving our lives and the lives of our children and grandchildren! And He did this because He loved us. We need to turn from being negative to being positive. Knowing the truth God spoke to us through the life of Joseph is the only way to make that change.

5

Origination of the Different Races

There have been countless opinions as to where the different races of men came from and how they originated. Truth, however, is found only in the Word of God. While praying to the Father, Jesus said, **Your word is truth** (John 17:17).

Let's go back to the very beginning of man. God created the first man and woman — Adam and Eve. Genesis 2:7 says, **The Lord God formed the man from the dust of the ground and breathed into his nostrils the breath of life, and the man became a living being.**

Man's body was handcrafted by God. The word *formed* means to squeeze into shape, to mold into form as an artist.[1] Man and woman were both works of art!

Man's body was made of dry earth or soil. The Hebrew word for *soil* means clay, loam, not fine dust.[2]

Adam's body was made from the ground. Here is where we get some clues as to his color. The words *man* and *Adam* are the same word in the Hebrew language and they mean "red."[3] Since Adam's body was made from the soil, we know this "red" could not be fire engine red. There is no fire engine red dirt. Since there is no white dirt, we know he was not reddish-white. Dirt is brown to black. Therefore, Adam was reddish-brown, having been made with red clay from the earth.

Eve was taken out of the reddish-brown man, Adam. She was reddish-brown and is called "red" or "man." *Man* means red. (Gen. 5:1,2.)

Only Adam's body was made from the reddish-brown dirt. His inner man, his personality, intellect, emotions, will and spirit were not made with dirt but with the breath of God. God breathed into this reddish-brown dirt, and a living person came into existence.

Only on the outside are we different colors. Inside, we are all created with the very same breath of God. Should we not major on the breath of God that fills every man, instead of the shade of dirt our bodies are made from?

Adam and Eve had children. What color were they? They were reddish-brown, like their parents. In fact, mankind had only one color until the birth of Noah's sons. Everyone was reddish-brown.

Different races of men did not exist before the flood of Noah. Genesis 5:1 says, **This is the written account of Adam's line**. We could read the verse like this, "This is the lineage of the man who was reddish-brown." *Adam* means red, soil red or brown red. If this is the account of the man who is reddish-brown, then everyone in this line must be reddish-brown. This chapter contains the names of Adam, Seth, Enosh, Kenan, Mahalalel, Jared, Enoch, Methuselah, Lamech and Noah. All of these men were reddish-brown, like their ancestors, Adam and Eve. We have no clue in the Bible that the color of man changed until Shem, Ham and Japheth were born.

Noah is listed as part of the line of the "red" man, Adam. Noah and his wife must therefore be reddish-brown, too. But something awesome happened when this reddish-brown couple had children. *They had three sons, each a different color!* Shem was dark olive-complected, Ham was black and Japheth was white. Shem was the first olive-complected man ever born. Ham was the first black man ever born. Japheth was the first Caucasian or white man ever born.

Listed below are the names of Noah and his family and what their names mean in the original Hebrew language:[4]

Noah - Rest, comfort

Shem - Celebrated, distinguished, a celebrated name

Ham - Black

Japheth - Enlargement

Permit me to digress a little here and talk about Cain and Abel, because some have erroneously said that the "mark of Cain" created the black race. Adam and Eve had three children — Cain, Abel and Seth. Cain murdered his brother Abel and was punished by the Lord for his crime. Some have ignorantly and maliciously used this story to proclaim their version of the origin of the black race.

After the murder of Abel, God said to Cain, **Now you are under a curse and driven from the ground...When you work the ground, it will no longer yield its crops for you. You will be a restless wanderer on the earth** (Gen. 4:11,12). Cain answered the Lord by saying, **My punishment is more than I can bear. Today you are driving me from the land, and I will be hidden from your presence; I will be a restless wanderer on the earth, and whoever finds me will kill me** (Gen. 4:13,14).

Cain was worried that someone was going to kill him, but God reassured him this would not happen. God said, **Not so; if anyone kills Cain, he will suffer**

vengeance seven times over. Then the Lord put a mark on Cain so that no one who found him would kill him (Gen. 4:15).

It has been said that God turned Cain into a black man as a curse and punishment for his sin. This is a false statement that has been leveled against a race of people loved by God and created in His image.

The punishment of Cain was banishment from the ground he worked and from the presence of the Lord. (Gen. 4:13-15.) The mark God put on Cain was not part of the punishment. It was a mark to protect him. It was a mark of mercy, not a curse. If being black was the mark, then being black is a direct result of the mercy and goodness of God.

One reason the story of Cain was connected with black people is that people have erroneously associated the color "black" with negative connotations. Many people assume that the symbolic color of sin and evil is black, while white supposedly symbolizes purity. Not so! God tells us in Isaiah 1:18 that the color of sin is scarlet red. **Though your sins are like *scarlet*, they shall be as white as snow**.

The Bible also mentions the color of Satan, **Then another sign appeared in heaven: an enormous *red* dragon with seven heads and ten horns and seven crowns on his heads** (Rev. 12:3). **The great dragon was hurled down — that ancient serpent called the devil, or Satan** (Rev. 12:9).

Biblically, the color of black does not symbolize anything sinful, wicked or evil. The color of red represents sin and Satan.

Now let's get back to Noah and his three sons. From Shem, Ham and Japheth **came the people who were**

scattered over the earth (Gen. 9:19). Every human being on planet earth is a direct descendant of Noah and is blood-related to Shem, Ham or Japheth. That means we are all blood cousins. God **hath made of one blood all nations of men for to dwell on all the face of the earth** (Acts 17:26 KJV). We may have different colors and shades of skin, but we are all one blood. The same blood courses through the veins of all humans — black, white, yellow or brown.

We also have a common genealogy. Regardless of color, the great men listed in Genesis 5 are the beginning of your personal family tree. This is not only Adam's line, but it is your line. These men are your great, great, great...grandfathers. Noah is the last relative that we all have in common. Regardless of race, if you could trace your family genealogy back far enough, you would eventually come to Noah. Every person alive today is a direct descendant of Noah. This means that all men are related. Scripture says, **Ascribe to the Lord,** *O families* **of nations, ascribe to the Lord glory and strength** (Ps. 96:7). The nations of the world are all related and part of the same family.

Shem, Noah's olive-complexioned son, became the father of the Arabs, Jews, Persians, Assyrians, Aramaeans and the western nations of Asia. (Gen. 10:21-31.) Abraham, Isaac and Jacob are descended from Shem. The dark olive-complexioned people of the Middle East and the Asians can trace their ancestry to Shem. Shem has a very distinguished place, because he is listed in the genealogy of the Lord Jesus Christ. (Luke 3:36.) Like His Jewish predecessors, Jesus Christ was a direct descendant of Shem.

The sons of Shem: Elam, Asshur, Arphaxad, Lud and Aram (Gen. 10:22).

Josephus says that Elam was the founder of the Persians.

Asshur is the father of the Assyrians.

The people of Israel are descended from Arphaxad. (Luke 3:36.)

Lud founded the Ludim of Asia Minor.

There is no doubt that Shem is connected to the olive-complected people of the Middle East.

Ham was a black man. We know this because the Hebrew word for *Ham* means black.[5] Ham was not cursed black, he was born black by the will of God.

Ham became the father of the people of Egypt and Africa. Psalm 105:23 says, **Then Israel entered Egypt; Jacob lived as an alien** *in the land of Ham*.

Ham had four sons. **The sons of Ham: Cush, Mizraim, Put and Canaan** (Gen. 10:6). Only one of the sons was cursed, and that was Canaan. (Gen. 9:25.) Since Ham was black, naturally all four of his sons were black.

Now, let's look at the names of the sons of Ham:[6]

Cush - A black countenance, Greek, Ethiopia

Mizraim - Two-fold Egypt

Put - Extension

Canaan - Merchant, servant, to be humbled, to be subdued, to be brought low.

At this particular time in Biblical history, a person's name revealed the most important truth or characteristic about that person, his vocation or life. Names are the most important clues we have about many of the individuals in the Bible. Many times names were even prophetic. Such was the case with Noah, whose name means "comfort" and Abraham, which means "father of a multitude."

Cush, like his father, was a black man. He became the father of the black people of Ethiopia. Ham, Cush and their black African descendants were never cursed. They were never told they were to be slaves.

Mizraim was the founder of Egypt. He was not cursed.

Put founded Libya in northern Africa. He was not included in Noah's curse.

Canaan, the slave, though black, never dwelt in Africa but in the area of Palestine. Because of the curse upon him and his descendants, his land was given to Abraham, Isaac and Jacob — the people of Israel.

In Matthew 15:21-28, the Lord Jesus ministered to a black Canaanite woman. This woman was under the curse of Noah. She pressed Jesus for a miracle of deliverance for her daughter. Not only did Jesus give this black lady what she asked for, but He said she had great faith! In responding to this Canaanite woman, Jesus reversed the curse of Noah!

Japheth, the white son of Noah, was the forefather of the Europeans. The white race can trace their ancestry to him. In Genesis 10:2, Japheth's sons are listed as **Gomer, Magog, Madai, Javan, Tubal, Meshech and Tiras**. Their descendants settled to the north and to the west in what is now Europe.

Gomer is the founder of the Cimbrians and most of the western nations of Europe. Camden thinks that the ancient Britons came from him, because they call themselves Kumero, Cymro and Kumeri, which seems to denote them as the posterity of Gomer.[7]

Magog fathered the Scythians and Tartars.[8]

Madai is the founder of the Medes.[9]

Javan settled in Greece, Achaia and the countries around it, including Macedonia and the regions of the west. He was the father of the Ionians, and this name is used metonymically for the Greeks and their country. The prophet Daniel calls Alexander, who came out of Macedonia, king of Javan, which the English version translates Greece.[10] The Greeks were first known by the name "Javan."[11]

Tiras' descendants possessed the northern part of Europe and peopled Thracia and Mysia.[12]

How is it possible for Noah and his wife to have three sons, each of a different color? We are dealing with a supernatural call of God on an entire family to go forth and replenish the earth. Remember, Noah, Shem, Ham and Japheth were uniquely blessed of God to save the human race and repopulate the earth. (Gen. 9:1.) Noah and his wife were functioning under the supernatural call, blessing and covenant of God. Since God is the Creator and is all-powerful, He can create whatever He wants. Colossians 1:16 says, **For by him all things were created...all things were created by him and for him.** Revelation 4:11 again echos this truth: **For you created all things, and by your will they were created and have their being.**

Scientifically, it is possible for black or dark parents to produce, not only black offspring, but also white. Genetically, white can come out of black, but black cannot come out of white. Therefore, Noah and his wife could have three sons, each of a different color.

Sometimes scientific evidence surfaces that proclaims one race more intelligent than another. I refute that, because it goes against Biblical truth and principles. If all men are created in the image and likeness of God, then all are intelligent. How a person develops their intelligence is an individual matter, not a racial one.

There are many flaming racial arrows shot in this world. Some are launched even by science. Stick to what you know to be truth from the Word of God.

Of greater value than any scientific explanation is the simple, yet profound, truth of the Bible that mankind was created by God, for God and in the likeness of God. God created black people in His image, white people in His image and olive-complected people in His image. Color itself really is inconsequential.

Where did the different races of men come from? They each came from God through Noah and his wife. Each race was sovereignly designed by God. God used Noah and his wife to save the human race and bring forth something new on the earth after the flood. God planned a new world with men who would be of different colors and shades. It was never His intent that the various colors would war with each other, separate from one another and debase one another.

Let's stop putting people down. When you put down another human being, you are actually attacking the very image of God. You are smearing the likeness of God. I believe God takes it as a personal insult when we put down His likeness in a man.

God instituted the law of murder, because He saw the killing of another human being as an attack upon Himself. **Whoever sheds the blood of man, by man shall his blood be shed;** *for in the image of God has God made man* (Gen. 9:6).

When we attack man — verbally or physically — we are attacking God's image. When you put down people because of their color, you are attacking the God

Who created them. Everyone deserves to be respected, because it is God's image they bear.

If you look down on black people, you are looking down on the likeness of God. If you demean white people, you are demeaning the likeness of God. If you degrade Hispanic people, you are degrading God's resemblance. It is time we realize how much we have sinned against the Lord and repent.

God loves people — all people. God is "up" on everyone and "down" on no one. Make that your personal philosophy. Be up on people — all people. Don't be up on some and down on others. Be like your heavenly Father. Speak well of all people.

> For out of the overflow of the heart the mouth speaks.
>
> The good man brings good things out of the good stored up in him, and the evil man brings evil things out of the evil stored up in him.
>
> But I tell you that men will have to give account on the day of judgment for every careless word they have spoken.
>
> For by your words you will be acquitted, and by your words you will be condemned.
>
> Matthew 12:34-37

Stop joking about races, ethnic groups and nationalities. Man is not a joke. Such joking keeps prejudice alive and reveals the evil things that are still in the heart.

Remember, the same breath of God that created you created all people. Our bodies may be different colors and shades, but inside, where it really counts, we are all made out of the same thing — the life of God!

Let's stop making such a big issue out of mud!

6
Prejudice

Prejudice is nothing new, nor has America cornered the market on it. Unfortunately, people all over the world are prejudiced in some way. Racism is universal.

Look at the word *prejudice*. It is made up of three syllables: "prej," "u," and "dice." The prefix *pre* means "before" and judice means "judge" or "judgment."[1] *Prejudice* is therefore passing judgment or forming an opinion about a person before you meet them or before you know them.

One reason we make these "pre" judgments is because of stereotyping. Stereotyping is categorizing everyone of a certain race as being "just alike." What a misnomer! If you had a bad experience with one black person, then you believe that all black people are just like the one you had the bad experience with. If you encountered a terribly biased white person, then you feel that all white people are alike. *All black people are not alike! All white people are not alike!* All races of people contain the good, the bad and the ugly, but don't call all bad or ugly. Do not pre-judge a whole race because you have had a few bad experiences.

In talking about racial prejudice, let's begin with *honesty*. Proverbs says, **He who conceals his sins does not prosper, but whoever confesses and renounces them finds mercy** (Prov. 28:13). Let us be truthful and admit that in some way and to some degree, we are all prejudiced.

You can always tell when someone is prejudiced because they are the first to say, "I am not prejudiced, but...."

You may not be conscious of it, but the right circumstances could expose your prejudice. If you are white, what would you do if black people bought all the houses on your street? You don't even know these people, but most would have a "For Sale" sign in front of their house within hours. If you are black, what would you do if white people bought all the houses on your street? I suspect another "For Sale" sign would go up. You see, we can all be prejudiced.

Much of the prejudice that lives in our minds and hearts was put there by someone else. That's right, someone taught you to be prejudiced. Someone planted prejudice in you. Someone told you negative things about black or white people. It could have been parents, grandparents, relatives or friends. Even preachers, deacons and Sunday school teachers could have contributed to the prejudice that you now find in your heart.

White people are not the only people who are prejudiced. Black people are prejudiced, too. So are many other ethnic groups and nationalities. The truth is that inside every white person lives a little "Archie Bunker," and inside every black person lives a little "George Jefferson." We all have our "Archie" or "George" to deal with.

As Christians, we need to understand that prejudice is one of the works of the flesh. Listen to what Paul said in Galatians 5:19-21:

The acts of the sinful nature are obvious: sexual immorality, impurity and debauchery;

Idolatry and witchcraft; hatred, discord, jealousy, fits of rage, selfish ambition, dissensions, factions

And envy; drunkenness, orgies, and the like. I warn you, as I did before, that those who live like this will not inherit the kingdom of God.

Hatred is the ultimate expression of prejudice. The Greek word for *hatred* literally means enmity or hostility. Synonyms for enmity and hostility are: animosity, bitterness, hatred, antagonism, belligerence, conflict, battle and war.[2] If there is any animosity or bitterness in your heart toward the white race, the black race, the Asian people or any other ethnic group, you are walking in the flesh! Obviously, the Holy Spirit is not hostile, so it must be the flesh. It is the sinful nature within us that is hostile. Wake up, dear Christian and realize that hostility is not of God!

Realize also, you don't fight hostility with hostility. The world says to fight fire with fire, but that is not true in the Kingdom of God. You don't combat prejudice with prejudice, hate with hate and bitterness with bitterness. You don't fight anger with anger. That is how the lost people of the world handle situations. When you handle conflicts like the world, war erupts. As Christians, we are called to make war on the devil, not on people.

Discord in the Greek means strife, contention, quarrels, rivalries. Prejudice produces strife and contention. It results in quarrels. Synonyms for *strife, contentions* and *quarrels* are: conflict, friction, clash, struggle, contend, differ, disagree, oppose, complaint, dispute.[3] If you have a quarrel in your heart with black people or white people, you are in the flesh.

Proverbs 17:19 says, **He who loves a quarrel loves sin**. Paul said to the Corinthians, **You are still worldly**.

For since there is jealousy and quarreling among you, are you not worldly? Are you not acting like mere men? (1 Cor. 3:3). Mere men cannot solve the racial problems of our day. It is going to take men and women who know God and who act according to the Spirit of God to make a difference. **A gentle answer turns away wrath, but a harsh word stirs up anger** (Prov. 15:1).

No wonder worldly people cannot get anywhere with problems. They are handling them in the flesh. Flesh, however, cannot solve problems, heal schisms or manifest love.

Fits of rage mean great anger, wrath, rage and passion. If you are angry with races, ethnic groups and nationalities, you are walking in the flesh. Many carry a continuous anger in their heart towards certain groups of people. Then, they pass their anger on to their children.

Dissensions literally mean "standing apart." Unfortunately in our great nation, we see people standing apart, fighting and accusing one another. Even in the house of God, people are standing apart from one another. We are not much better than the world when it comes to being delivered from prejudice. We have black churches, white churches and Korean churches. The prophetic move of God for the future is to break down these fleshly barriers so that each local church will be open to everyone, regardless of color or race.

Some cities even have two First Baptist Churches: the white First Baptist Church and the black First Baptist Church. In the near future, the Spirit of God is going to so move that there will be only one First Baptist Church; and it will be comprised of both blacks and whites who love the Lord Jesus and one another. Any church that refuses this move of God is going to be left behind as the Spirit moves on. Don't be surprised to see the words, *Ichabod, the glory has departed*, over the doors of some churches.

The time for standing apart is over! God is calling His true people together, to be one in Christ. Color doesn't mean a thing!

Have you ever wondered why black brothers and sisters have to go to a different church than you go to? Or, why white brothers and sisters have to go to another church?

It's time we realize that we need one another. With all hell breaking loose on planet earth, it is not time to separate. It's time to come together in Jesus so that we can draw on each others' strengths, share each others' gifts and walk in the agreement taught by Jesus in Matthew 18:19,20.

Prejudice is a work of the *sinful* nature. Whatever comes out of the sinful nature must therefore be sinful. It is sinful to be prejudiced! It is natural for the lost people of the world to walk in prejudice. After all, they are lost and without Christ. We cannot expect much more out of lost people than lost behavior. It is another matter, though, when a child of God is prejudiced. If Christ is in you, the love of Christ for all men should be coming out of you!

Prejudice is unholy! I don't like hypocritical holiness. Many Christians are praying for a return to the holiness of God. To them, *holiness* means nothing more than not watching television or going to the movies. To others, it means not wearing jewelry, makeup or lipstick. If you really want to see how holy you are, take a look at how you feel about black people or white people. Your racial attitudes reveal your true level of holiness, much more so than whether or not you watch "Leave It to Beaver." Makeup, lipstick and cigarettes are shallow indicators of holiness in comparison to racial prejudice.

If you are prejudiced, you are unholy. Some say, "I can't help it. I'm just a prejudiced Christian." That's like saying, "I can't help it, I'm an adulterous Christian," or "I'm a lying Christian." Prejudice is a force of evil that is contrary to Christ. You will never be holy until it is removed from your heart and mind.

While some are majoring on the unholiness of cigarettes, which is a defilement of the body, how much more should we major on the unholiness of prejudice, which is a defilement of the heart.

It's hypocritical to say, "I'm holy, I quit drugs," when in your heart you hate white people. It is equally hypocritical to say, "I'm holy, I broke off that immoral relationship," when in your heart you hate black people.

Some prejudice is so deep that it goes beyond the flesh and is demonic. These demons live in certain people, black and white, and manifest themselves in hatred, anger, hostility and murder. If your prejudice is so strong that it cannot be crucified with Christ, then it is demonic and must be cast out!

Prejudice within the human heart is certainly not a manifestation of the Holy Spirit! Repent! Let God clean you up and give you a true love for all people.

The Scriptures are plain. Christians are called to minister to all men. First Timothy 2:3,4 says, **This is good, and pleases God our Savior, who wants *all men to be saved* and to come to a knowledge of the truth.** If God wants all men to be saved, why are you ministering only to white men, black men or Korean men?

In the gospel of Mark, Jesus says, **Go ye into all the world, and preach the gospel to** *every creature* (Mark 16:15 KJV). If we are to preach the good news about Jesus to *every person*, why are we preaching only to black people or white people? The Great Commission is colorblind! Are you?

In Acts 6:1, we learn that the very first argument within the early church was a racial one. *The King James Version* puts it this way: **There arose a murmuring of the Grecians against the Hebrews, because their widows were neglected in the daily ministration**. The Greeks felt that their widows were being neglected because they were Greek and that the Hebrew widows were being given special treatment because they were Hebrew. This incident shows that prejudice is nothing new.

Peter learned a great lesson about prejudice. God had to speak to him supernaturally because he, as a typical Jew, was very prejudiced against all non-Jews. The story is told in Acts 10. It involves a man by the name of Cornelius. Cornelius was not a Jew. In fact, he was an Italian. He was **a centurion in what was known as the Italian Regiment** (Acts 10:1). **He and all his family were devout and God-fearing; he gave generously to those in need and prayed to God regularly** (Acts 10:2).

Notice that Cornelius, though a Gentile, believed in God, gave money and prayed regularly. Here is an important truth. Even though Cornelius believed in God, gave money and prayed, he was lost. He had not heard the Gospel of Jesus Christ and therefore had not believed in the Lord Jesus.

This story shows us that belief in the existence of God does not save you. It is faith in the Son of God,

Jesus Christ, that saves a person. However, God did honor the prayers and offerings of Cornelius. In response, God gave Cornelius a vision, instructing him to send men to Joppa to bring back Simon Peter. (Acts 10:3-6). The next day, as Peter went to prayer:

> He became hungry and wanted something to eat, and while the meal was being prepared, he fell into a trance.
>
> He saw heaven opened and something like a large sheet being let down to earth by its four corners.
>
> It contained all kinds of four-footed animals, as well as reptiles of the earth and birds of the air.
>
> Then a voice told him "Get up, Peter. Kill and eat."
>
> "Surely not, Lord!" Peter replied. "I have never eaten anything impure or unclean."
>
> The voice spoke to him a second time, "Do not call anything impure that God has made clean."
>
> This happened three times, and immediately the sheet was taken back to heaven.
>
> **Acts 10:10-16**

After Peter watched this happen three different times, three Gentile men were knocking at the door to take him back to Cornelius. This vision was not about clean and unclean food. It was about *people*, Gentile people.

The Jews believed that Gentiles were unclean and excluded from the love of God and the salvation of Jesus Christ. In that day and time and in that culture, the Jews believed that every Gentile man, woman, boy and girl was a dirty pagan dog. They would not touch a Gentile, eat with a Gentile or go into a Gentile's house. They thought all Gentiles were base, foul persons who would contaminate them. The racial prejudice between Jews and Gentiles was horrific.

No wonder it took a supernatural vision from God to deal with the prejudice in Peter and prepare him to go to a Gentile's home to share the Gospel. If Peter had not had this vision, he would not have gone to Cornelius' house, simply because Cornelius was a Gentile and, therefore, unclean.

Peter said to Cornelius and his family, **You are well aware that it is against our law for a Jew to associate with a Gentile or visit him. But God has shown me that I should not call any man impure or unclean** (Acts 10:28).

Thank God, Peter was delivered from his long-standing prejudice. However, not everyone saw the vision Peter saw. When Peter went to Jerusalem, those who were still prejudiced criticized him. **So when Peter went up to Jerusalem, the circumcised believers criticized him and said, "You went into the house of uncircumcised men and ate with them"** (Acts 11:2,3). People, black and white, who have been freed from prejudice can expect criticism and persecution from those who are still prejudiced.

The Lord Jesus was not prejudiced when He walked this earth and ministered to hurting humanity. You will recall the story of Jesus and the woman at the well. (John 4.) For Jesus to reach this woman with the message of eternal life, He had to cross three major barriers.

First, He crossed the gender barrier. Usually, men did not talk to women, especially Samaritan women. No wonder this woman said, **You are a Jew and I am a Samaritan woman. How can you ask me for a drink?** (John 4:9).

Second, Jesus crossed the racial barrier. **For Jews do not associate with Samaritans** (John 4:9). Samaritans were hated by the Jews. They were a mix of Jewish and Gentile blood and theologically were a blend of Jewish doctrine and paganism. They were despised outcasts, but Jesus did not care! He stepped over the racial line to reach this woman with His love.

Third, there was the religious barrier. This woman was not only divorced and remarried; she was divorced five times and was presently living with her sixth male companion. There are preachers, churches and denominations today that would not cross that barrier to get this woman saved. Jesus loves people, all people, and will cross any obstacle to make them His own. Should we not be like Jesus?

Even in His death, Jesus broke down racial barriers and brought people together.

> **For he himself is our peace, who has made the two one and has destroyed the barrier, the dividing wall of hostility.**
>
> **His purpose was to create in himself one new man out of the two, thus making peace,**
>
> **And in this one body to reconcile both of them to God through the cross, by which he put to death their hostility.**
>
> Ephesians 2:14-16

In context, this passage is talking about Jews and Gentiles, but in principle, it can apply to other areas of racial segregation as well. Jesus has made the two, one. All segregation is over. Jesus is building only one new man in the earth. This one new man is comprised of all born-again people: Jews, Gentiles, black, white, rich, poor, males and females. Jesus is building us together, to be His one and only bride. We believers are the bride of Christ. There is no white bride or black bride, only Jesus' blood-washed bride.

Let's take a closer look at the phrase, *the dividing wall of hostility* (Eph. 2:14). Hostility in a person's heart is the dividing wall between people and races. Hostility is what separates people, but Jesus takes hostility out of the human heart. How can we therefore be divided? The hostility we once had toward black people or white people is now gone. It was that hostility that kept us apart from one another, but without hostility, there is no more wall, no more separation. The presence of Jesus within a person tears down the barriers of hostility and anger.

If hostility has not been removed out of your heart, even your salvation is questionable. If you still have hostile thoughts and feelings toward black people or white people, it is doubtful that the new nature of Christ dwells within you. The nature of Christ is a nature of love and good will toward men. (Luke 2:14 KJV.)

Prejudice is the reason some churches are not racially mixed. Some would say, "Blacks are welcome in our church," but where? On the back pew? Can a black man be a pastor, elder or deacon in your church? Will the white members receive a black pastor? Can the black brother serve on the church board? Can a black brother or sister be in the choir or band? What would happen if your choir or band was comprised of more blacks than whites? What if more blacks start coming to your church than whites? If you're really not prejudiced, it won't matter to you.

God has called us to minister to people, not some people, but *all* people. God never authorized us to pick and choose the people we wanted to minister to. All people are dearly loved in God's sight, and if you are a true child of God, they will be dearly loved in your sight.

What about churches that are all black? Do they have any white members? If not, why not? If there are white members, can they be a minister in the church? Can they be on the board? If a lot of white people started coming to your church, what then? If you love people, you will want white people in your church.

Black churches should not be built on a black brotherhood. No church has the right or authority from heaven to be an exclusive club. Do we have invisible signs over our church doors that say, "For Whites Only"? Do we have attitudes in place that say, "For Blacks Only"?

Just as God had to get prejudice out of Peter, so He has to get it out of all of us. It does take God to get prejudice out of people. That is why all political and sociological attempts to get prejudice and hatred out of the hearts of men will fail. It cannot be done though legislation. We don't need a new law. We need a change of heart and mind that only God can give through relationship with Jesus Christ. Politicians and sociologists cannot do the job, but Jesus can! Yes, knowing Jesus is the only real answer to racial problems.

If you belong to Christ, He will work in your heart, and all the faster if you open your heart to His truth. Quit justifying your prejudice. Repent of it. It is a sin. No man is unclean because of his racial or ethnic background, but prejudice in the heart of a man makes him unclean. Jesus said:

> **What comes out of a man is what makes him "unclean."**
>
> **For *from within*, out of men's hearts, come evil thoughts, sexual immorality, theft, murder, adultery,**

Greed, malice, deceit, lewdness, envy, slander, arrogance and folly.

All these evils come *from inside* and make a man unclean.

Mark 7:20-23

Let me state again, in this matter of racial prejudice, we must quit stereotyping. I own a Rottweiler. Rottweilers are big dogs, easily weighing over one hundred pounds. They are thought of as vicious killers, but my dog is a kitty cat. She crawls up into my lap and would rather be petted than eat. Because she is a Rottweiler, people assume she is mean. They have stereotyped her. She will never get a fair shake in this world, because all Rottweilers have been stereotyped as being ferocious. All Rottweilers are not ferocious, but people think they are.

On the other hand, my close friend owned a Cocker Spaniel. Cockers are thought of as being friendly family dogs, but his Cocker was mean. They had to get rid of him because of his tendency to bite. If dogs can be unfairly stereotyped, what about men? How much worse it is to categorize people. All people are not the same!

Understand, too, there are different classes of people within every race. Every race has its high class, middle class and low class. There are high class black people and low class white people, and there are high class white people and low class black people.

Once I went to Washington, DC, to pray for our country. As I walked around the White House, I turned the corner and came upon Pennsylvania Avenue. Just as I did, a white man living in a cardboard box, right in front of the White House, pulled out a brand new fifth of whiskey from a brown paper bag. Does that mean that every white person is like that? Right across the street from him, in the park, was a black man sleeping on a bench in a cardboard box. Does that mean that every black person is like that?

When God gets prejudice out of your heart, some people who are close to you may not like it. A certain camaraderie is built around the fact that we do not like black or white people. When God sets you free, others may not desire your company, because what God has done in you makes them look bad.

7

The Brotherhood of Believers

There are only two families in the earth, spiritually speaking. There is the family of God, which is comprised of all people all over the world who have been born again through faith in Jesus Christ and have therefore received the indwelling of the Holy Spirit. **And if anyone does not have the Spirit of Christ, he does not belong to Christ** (Rom. 8:9). Then, there is the family of lost people, who have not accepted Christ but have the spirit of this world.

As for you, you were dead in your transgressions and sins,

In which you used to live when you followed the ways of this world and of the ruler of the kingdom of the air, *the spirit who is now at work in those who are disobedient.*

Ephesians 2:1,2

These Scriptures talk about two different spirits — the Spirit of Christ and the spirit of the ruler of the kingdom of the air. Every human being is influenced by one of these spirits. Christians are influenced by the Holy Spirit, and lost people are influenced by the spirit of the world.

Jesus recognized these different spirits and said to one group of people, **You belong to your father, the devil, and you want to carry out your father's desire**

73

(John 8:44). People are more related by spirit than by skin.

Jesus made it clear that the spiritual family of God took precedence over the natural family of the flesh. Of course, your natural family may also be part of the spiritual family of God. Hopefully they are. Nonetheless, here's what the Bible says:

> While Jesus was still talking to the crowd, his mother and brothers stood outside, wanting to speak to him.
>
> Someone told him, "Your mother and brothers are standing outside, wanting to speak to you."
>
> He replied to him, "Who is my mother, and who are my brothers?"
>
> Pointing to his disciples, he said, "Here are my mother and my brothers.
>
> "For whoever does the will of my Father in heaven is my brother and sister and mother."
>
> **Matthew 12:46-50**

You see, God is the Creator of all men, but He is not the Father of all men! As believers, we should understand that we now belong to a new family, the family of God. (Gal. 6:10.) Because I have the Spirit of Christ, I am not related to all men anymore. This means that all black men are not "brothers." All Caucasian men are not "brothers." As a Christian, you are now related only to those who have like faith in Jesus and have the same Spirit that you have — the Holy Spirit.

I am not related to all Caucasians. Some white people are lost, possess the spirit of this world and the devil is their father. I am saved. I have the Holy Spirit and God is my Father.

There are black men and women who are saved, have the Holy Spirit and God is their Father. Who am I related to, lost white people or saved black people? Or, if I'm black, am I related to lost black people or saved white people?

It boils down to this, are you brother to a lost person? Why would you call a lost man your "brother" just because he has the same color of skin that you have? Black people are especially bad about calling all black people "brother" or "sister." This black brotherhood must go if you're a Christian, because as a born-again person, you are no longer related to everyone who is black. Now that you are a Christian, you are in brotherhood to all Christians all over the world, regardless of color, nationality or ethnic background. Relate more to grace than race!

Color no longer determines our brotherhood. The Spirit of Christ determines who we are in brotherhood with. So everyone is not your brother. Only those who do the will of the heavenly Father. God has not called us to a black brotherhood or a white brotherhood. He has called us to *a brotherhood of believers*! Scripture says, **Love the brotherhood of believers** (1 Pet. 2:17). Some build a brotherhood around being poor or rich. Others build a brotherhood around being persecuted and mistreated. Still, there are brotherhoods built on secret oaths. *This is flesh!* The only brotherhood God has authorized and recognized is the brotherhood of believers. Jesus is the Head of that brotherhood.

It's time that believers walk in the truth of the Lord Jesus Christ. New Testament relationships are relationships of grace, not race! Grace is more important than race. Grace is of God and belongs to the born-again man. Race is of God, too, but belongs to the natural man.

Something happened to us at salvation that we have never quite captured. Our earthly racial identities died at the foot of the cross, and we received a brand new identity as sons and daughters of God. Colossians 3:11 puts it this way: **Here there is no Greek or Jew, circumcised or uncircumcised, barbarian, Scythian, slave or free, but Christ is all, and is in all.**

If you were a Gentile and came to Christ, you did not become a saved Gentile. You became a Christian, a child of God, part of the family of God. You are no longer a Gentile! If people asked you what you were, you would not answer, "a Gentile." You would answer, "A Christian." There is no such thing as a Christian Gentile. You are either a Christian or a Gentile, but you cannot be both! A Gentile is what you were before Christ. A new creation is what you are after Christ. **Therefore, if anyone is in Christ, he is a new creation; the old has gone, the new has come!** (2 Cor. 5:17).

Galatians 3:26-28 speaks forth the same truth:

> **You are all sons of God through faith in Christ Jesus,**
>
> **For all of you who were baptized into Christ have clothed yourselves with Christ.**
>
> **There is neither Jew nor Greek, slave nor free, male nor female,** *for you are all one in Christ Jesus.*

When we come to Christ, we lose our racial identities. Our identity is no longer "black" or "white." It is "Christian."

If the Lord Jesus appeared in the sky and made the following three statements, which one would you obey? If He pointed to the sky and said, "I want all white people to assemble in the west, I want all black people to assemble in the east and I want all Christians to assemble in the north," which direction would you run? Are you black, white or Christian? If you're white, then act white. If you're black, then act black. But if you're Christian, then act Christian!

Something else that died at the cross of Christ was our worldly "purposes" and "causes" for living. Many black people feel that they should fight for "the cause." What cause? The cause of racial equality? That is not the purpose of the Christian. All Christians have purpose. Black and white alike, we have the same purpose. Jesus has given us a "cause" to live for. Our cause is the Great Commission. Don't let lost people put their worldly causes on you. As noble and needed as some of those causes are, we cannot get distracted from the cause of Christ. We desperately need racial equality, but what better way to achieve it than by getting men and women born again. Only as Christ moves in and has His way does prejudice move out. As new creations, we must major on getting people saved and teaching them the Word of God. It takes the Word to change a person and build the nature of God into him.

For too long Christians have fought racial battles with the weapons of this world. As a Christian:

> We do not wage war as the world does.
>
> The weapons we fight with are not the weapons of the world. On the contrary, they have divine power to demolish strongholds.
>
> We demolish arguments and every pretension that sets itself up against the knowledge of God, and we take captive every thought to make it obedient to Christ.
>
> 2 Corinthians 10:3-5

Our weapons have divine power! We need to use the weapons of Jesus to pull down racial strongholds. When encountering a person who is prejudiced, start dealing with the evil spirit that is controlling and speaking through the person. Christians are to fight demons but love people. We don't love demons and fight people!

One night, just as I laid my head on my pillow and closed my eyes, the gift of discerning of spirits was manifested by the Holy Spirit. I saw a demon! It was dressed like a clown, with a clown-type collar around its neck and a pointed hat on its head. The color of this demon was split right down the middle. The left half of it was black and the right half of it was white. The Holy Spirit spoke to me and said, "This is the spirit of racial division, and it has come to cause dissension between the black and white people of your church."

The spirit of racial division incites one people against another. It magnifies differences and focuses people's attention on those differences. This evil spirit focuses us on "race" instead of "grace"! This demon works on both races, sowing suspicion and planting lies in the mind. Its main job and assignment from hell is to turn black against white and white against black.

When this demon is moving in a congregation, people will be so busy noticing what color the singers are that they will not be able to worship Jesus. Instead of focusing on Jesus, they will focus on the ethnic style of the music. If there are more black ushers than white or white than black, they will become disturbed and disgruntled.

Another manifestation of this spirit is that it lies to people. It says that people are prejudiced when they are not. It creates perceived division or an illusion of division. It can also create real division.

When this spirit is on people, they see everything through racial glasses and hear everything through racial hearing aids. When decisions are made in the church, they are not perceived spiritually. They are interpreted racially.

When this spirit is working, he must be brought down and *exposed*. Satan cannot stand to be exposed. He hates light. If you are a pastor, stand up in front of the congregation and tell them plainly that the spirit of racial division is working in the church. As you stand together as a local church, you can cast this spirit out in the name of Jesus.

You cannot fight demons with carnal weapons! You must have Holy Ghost power, the Word of God and the name and blood of Jesus. It's time we dealt with demons and not people!

Ephesians 6:12 says, **For our struggle is not against flesh and blood, but against the rulers, against the authorities, against the powers of this dark world and against** *the spiritual forces of evil* **in the heavenly realms.**

Even our racial struggle is not against flesh and blood. The devil is the one who is behind all racism. Lost nations cannot handle Satan, and lost people cannot handle him. It's time we focus our anger on the devil and do battle with him. Only then will we win!

If you're black, stop blaming white people for everything! It's time to get our eyes off of people. The devil is your real nemesis.

If you're white, stop blaming black people for everything! Black people are not your problem. Your enemy is the devil. (1 Pet. 5:8.)

Through Jesus Christ, God has done something very exciting. He has actually created a brand new race of men upon the earth. The Scriptures call believers a race. Speaking to the New Covenant believer, Scripture says:

> But you are a chosen people [race], a royal priesthood, a holy nation, a people belonging to God, that you may declare the praises of him who called you out of darkness into his wonderful light.
>
> Once you were not a people, but now you are the people of God.
>
> **1 Peter 2:9,10**

The Greek word for *people* in the above verse is "genos" and means "race." We could read the verse, "But you are a chosen race!" Yes, Christians are a race of people! You say, "But I'm black." You can't identify with both races. Which race do you want to identify with? Some would say, "I'm white," but you can't identify with both the white race and the Christian race. Since "Christian" is a new race of people to which all believers belong, we now identify with our new race and are related to "our own kind." Saved people are our people! Saved people are our own kind!

The Christian race is made up of people of all colors who love Jesus and have the Holy Spirit. The real brotherhood is not a skin brotherhood but a born-again brotherhood! Know who your real brothers are and love them all. Quit identifying with people who are not saved and therefore aren't your brothers and sisters. Reach out to them and attempt to bring them into the new family. They need to become like you. You don't need to become like them! **Bad company corrupts good character** (1 Cor. 15:33).

8

What's Wrong With Being Different?

Three times in the opening verses of 1 Corinthians 12, the word *different* is used. It says that there are *different* kinds of gifts, *different* kinds of service and *different* kinds of working. (1 Cor. 12:4-6.)

While it is not stated, it is obvious that there are also different kinds of people. Even within the same race, no two people are alike. That's the way God planned it. Only God could create six billion people and make them all different! When King Xerxes gave a banquet, the book of Esther says, **Wine was served in goblets of gold, each one different from the other** (Esth. 1:7). Every human being God has created is a goblet of gold! But even among goblets of gold, there are differences.

God is the great God of variety! All of nature testifies to this truth. The heavenly bodies, created and named by God Himself, are all different. **The sun has one kind of splendor, the moon another and the stars another; and star differs from star in splendor** (1 Cor. 15:41). There are countless stars in the universe, each one different from the others. God purposely made each one unique — one of a kind.

The plant world is the same way. Think of all the varieties and colors of plants, flowers, trees and shrubs.

The animal kingdom, with its multiple species, offers a beauty and uniqueness only God could have supplied. Even the insects are detailed and different in every corner of the globe. God is a God Who delights in variety! Why should we think that He would make all men alike?

Why do we human beings have a hard time with anyone who is different? We tend to withdraw from people who are not alike and criticize them. We have a tendency to collide with people who are different. Thus, people collide with people all over the world.

One thing that is different is our cultures. Black culture and white culture are different. One culture is not right and the other wrong. They are just different.

There are things about all cultures that are good and things that are sinful. Some characteristics and practices of all cultures are ungodly. As Christians, we must be delivered from the ungodly influences of our particular cultures. Everything about white culture is not Christian, and everything about black culture is not Christian.

Prejudice is even part of our culture. Prejudice against black people is part of our southern tradition and culture. Just recently, a black man went to the First Baptist Church in a small southern city. One church member, upon seeing the black visitor, got up and left the service. The congregation was so shaken that a board meeting was held immediately after the morning worship. Some are so proud of their southern heritage that they would rather be southern than saved!

The South, however, is not the only part of the United States that is prejudiced or has abused black people. A documentary revealed the discovery of a slave cemetery in downtown New York City. Black slaves were not just used on the plantations of the South. They were used in New York City, too.

The West is famous for its prejudice and abuse of the Asian people. Asians were worked mercilessly in building the great railroads.

All cultures have things in it that none of us should be proud of.

Look at Native American culture. Idolatry, witchcraft and demonology are integral parts of Native American culture. I believe that is one reason Native Americans have such a hard time getting saved. To accept Christ would necessitate a renouncing of their culture. If that's what it takes to accept Christ, so be it. Christ is more important than culture, and Christ takes precedence over culture. Christ is calling all people out of wickedness.

Christianity itself is a culture, a new culture. We need to identify with our new culture instead of our old one. Christ has indeed made us new creatures. How can new creatures live in old cultures?

Is there any value in being proud of our cultural heritage or color? Perhaps a little. What we really need is dignity. We do need to feel good about ourselves and our race. That is best accomplished through the Word of God and not the flesh.

There are many things about our racial cultures that are fine, and we do not need to get rid of those things. Black people don't need to become like white people, and white people don't need to become like black people. We all can keep the good parts of our respective cultures and pass them on to our children.

In 1 Corinthians 12, we learn the truth that different people in the Body of Christ have different gifts.

There are many gifts, and we all have one. That means I don't have it all! I may have a gift, but I don't have all gifts. That is one reason we need other people. Other people have gifts you don't have. They have strengths where you are weak, and you have strengths where they are weak. Therefore, don't collide with other people, but build a coalition with them.

God designed human beings to need one another. He also designed the Church the same way. Alone, we are just individuals, but together we are a team. One can chase a thousand, but two can put ten thousand to flight. (Deut. 32:30.) We need the very people we reject. The more people you reject and close yourself to, the more you are harming and limiting yourself. Don't throw people away just because they are different. Instead of threatening you, others who are different can enhance you.

Black people and white people need one another. We need to become a team. We can benefit from one anothers' gifts and be enriched by one anothers' cultures. It's better to be a team than to be opponents! We need coalition, not collision. Coalition is when different people reach out to one another, and without trying to change each other, hook arm and arm in joint support and true friendship. We need friends, not enemies. Let's quit colliding.

I once heard a minister reveal a truth that struck a cord with my spirit. He was speaking about the differences in the black and white form of worship. When blacks sing and worship, they clap their hands on the second and fourth beat of the measure. When white people praise God in song, they clap on the first and third beat. The richness of this is — *together* we don't miss a beat!

9

The Search for Dignity

My dignity is driven away as by the wind.

Job 30:15

Every human being is searching for dignity. That's because we all need self-respect. As beings created in the image and likeness of God, we have a God-given right to dignity.

Dignity is defined as "price, value, worth, significance, honor, recognition, respect and equality."[1] Possessing dignity makes you feel valuable, important and necessary. It means to have self-respect and honor, knowing that you are as valuable as any other person. Dignity causes you to feel good about who you are. We must all have this sense of self-worth and self-esteem!

Scripture, speaking of God's creation of man, says, **You made him [man] a little lower than the heavenly beings and crowned him with glory and honor** (Ps. 8:5). The English term, *heavenly beings*, is actually the translation of the Hebrew word, "Elohim."[2] "Elohim" is one of the names of God in the Old Testament. Genesis 1:1 says, **In the beginning God [Elohim] created the heavens and the earth**.

Psalm 8:5 actually reads, "You made him [man] a little lower than God." Think of it! Mankind was made just a little lower than God Himself! Man is not an animal. You did not evolve from apes and monkeys. You came from God and were made "just a little lower than God." God's order of creation would be: angels, man, animals, plants, insects, and so forth. Man is not in the animal classification. Man was created in the category of the heavenly beings.

God then crowned man with glory and honor! Glory and honor are our right, as creations of God. Every human being and every color of man has a right to this glory and honor. What a marvelous creation man is! Man is God's crowning achievement and was created full of dignity, beauty and respect. You should feel good about yourself!

One of Satan's biggest ploys is to make people not like themselves. Satan robs man of a positive self-image. Many people live their whole lives feeling condemned, inferior and no good. They do not like themselves or feel good about themselves. They lead negative lives of deep introspection and self-criticism. God made man with beauty and respect.

When Satan introduced sin into the world, one of his goals was to destroy man's dignity and self-esteem. Sin will destroy how you feel about yourself faster than anything. Sin demolishes dignity and self-respect. It kills all the positive feelings that you may have about yourself. **Sin is a disgrace to any people** (Prov. 14:34).

All people are searching for respect, appreciation and dignity. The women's movement was formed because women were looking for dignity and equality. Women are entitled to the glory, honor and dignity that belong to them as creations of God.

For women to have dignity, they do not have to dress like a man, talk like a man or drive a bulldozer. Dignity comes from who you are, not from what you do. Dignity is something that you have in your heart, not something derived by the work of your hands.

The various black movements that have risen within this country over the last 35 years are nothing more than black Americans seeking dignity, appreciation and respect, to which they are entitled.

Enslavement and prejudice did a lot more damage to black people than the obvious physical confinement. It damaged their dignity and marred their self-image. It destroyed their feelings of self-respect and importance. It planted in them the thoughts and feelings that, "There is something wrong with me," and that they are substandard and inferior to other men.

Our forefathers did not allow them to read or write. Slavery and prejudice told them that they were ignorant. Who can forget the days when a black person could not attend the state university to better himself and get an education? When black Americans tried to enroll their children in white schools, they were met with great opposition.

Black Americans were not allowed to vote, yet our Declaration of Independence stated, "All men are created equal and endowed with certain inalienable rights, among which are life, liberty and the pursuit of happiness." Black men and women could not even eat in a public restaurant or stay in a motel. We had "white" and "colored" restrooms and water fountains. Man stripped away the respect and dignity that God had bestowed.

Even today there are people still grappling over the old Confederate flag, a sign of slavery to many. Should it still fly over our state capitals? Of course not! Put it in a museum, but don't put it on the capital of my state. We already have a flag. It is the flag of the United States of America. That is the flag that unites us. That is the flag for which many have died. The flag of the United States is stained with the blood of all races and ethnic groups, who make us what we are: *One nation under God!*

But something happened in the 1960s. Black Americans said, "Enough is enough. We are as good as anybody. No longer will we go to the back of the bus. We want to eat in public restaurants, and we are going to get an education. Our children belong in school, and we are going to the universities. We want good jobs. We deserve to be treated with respect and equality!"

Voices arose among the black community. We did not understand them, or if we did, we didn't like what we heard. It was all a search for dignity, respect and self-esteem.

The image of God that is stamped on every man, woman and child cannot stand to be put down. Eventually, a volcano erupts inside a man when he has been made to feel substandard and inferior. God did not make people inferior or superior. He made us equal. Black people, created a little lower than God and crowned with glory and honor, exploded in righteous indignation. The Civil Rights Movement was born.

Even people like Malcolm X were just searching for dignity and respect. Some looked for dignity in the wrong places and in the wrong way. Nonetheless, that is what they were searching for.

Most white people don't understand what the "X" stands for when they see young black men wearing a cap or a T-shirt with the "X" on it. The "X" means, "We don't know who we really are."

Most black Americans carry white surnames that originated during times of slavery. I can understand how this can be an irritant, but the truth of the matter is that all of us, white as well as black, are a Mr. X.

Let me explain. Most of the time humans have been on this earth they did not have surnames (or last names). What was Adam's last name? He didn't have one. What about Noah? What was his surname? Abraham did not have a last name, neither did King David, Solomon, Isaiah, Daniel, Jeremiah, Mary, Joseph, Peter, Paul or John. No one in the Bible had a last name, including the Lord Jesus. Surnames came about centuries later when men "made up" their own last names. They took their last names mainly from their profession, location or a characteristic of their personality.

While you may be able to trace your ancestry back to a certain point, there will come a time, if you could go that far back, when there will be no surname and you will be a Mr. X. Regardless of race, your last name was simply "made up"! Whatever your surname is, you now have the opportunity to make it a name of dignity and honor. Your name will be what you make it!

Lost people are created in the image of God, and they are entitled to dignity, but they do not know where to get it. A lost world and a lost society are hardly the place to go for dignity. This world is steeped in sin, and sin destroys one's dignity. Only Jesus Christ can give a person true dignity, significance and self-worth!

Jesus does this by making you a new creature. Scripture says, **Therefore, if anyone is in Christ, he is a new creation; the old has gone, the new has come!** (2 Cor. 5:17). If you receive Him and call on His name, He makes you a son or daughter of God! (John 1:12.) The Holy Spirit literally moves into your spirit and takes up residence inside of you. Suddenly, you have a purpose for living, and everything in your life becomes new. Now, instead of being just black or white, you are related to the living God as a son or daughter of God! **Behold, what manner of love the Father hath bestowed upon us, that we should be called the sons of God** (1 John 3:1 KJV).

Dignity is something God gives you. **The Lord bestows favor and honor** (Ps. 84:11). It is something that you have on the inside. It is a deep inner knowing that you are as valuable as anyone else. With this sense of dignity, you could look the Queen of England right in the eye without any sense of inferiority! But better still, as children of God, we can now look God in the face without any sense of shame or humiliation. This is because of the blood of Jesus Christ. If we can approach the God of heaven with freedom and confidence, then most certainly we can approach any man on the face of the earth without feeling inferior.

You are inferior to no one. That's the way you should see yourself and feel about yourself. The blood of Jesus, the most precious substance in all of the universe, was given in order to bring you to heaven. God bought you. He paid for you. (1 Cor. 6:19,20.) The transaction for your soul was not a monetary one, because you are worth more than all the money in the world. Silver, gold, diamonds and rubies could not purchase you. There aren't enough of them. God set your value. You are so valuable to Him that He sent His Son, the second Person of the Holy Trinity, to die an agonizing death to bring you to heaven.

There are some interesting verses in 1 Corinthians 12 that teach the Church how to help people who have not been treated right by lost society.

First Corinthians 12:22-25 says:

On the contrary, those parts of the body that seem to be weaker are indispensable,

And the parts that we think are less honorable we treat with special honor. And the parts that are unpresentable are treated with special modesty,

While our presentable parts need no special treatment. But God has combined the members of the body and has given greater honor to the parts that lacked it,

So that there should be no division in the body, but that its parts should have equal concern for each other.

What a powerful teaching this is to the Church! You have to understand that the word *parts* means "people." There are people in the Church who "we think are less honorable." These people are not less honorable! Scripture does not say that they are less honorable. It says "we think" they are less honorable. These people have been treated wrongly by lost society. They have not been given the glory and honor rightfully due them. But when they come into the Church, God straightens this out. In the Church, these people receive *special honor*. Yes, some people in the Church should get special treatment. This passage of Scripture says so. People who have been "dishonored" by society are "given special honor" in the house of God. The passage says that God gives *greater honor* to the people who lacked it!

I have been accused of giving special honor to my black members. Perhaps I have, but they deserve it. Women also need special honor. Let's give honor to all and not leave anybody out. That is God's remedy and His healing.

The house of the Lord is a house of healing for all people. God knows what He is doing. Let's do things the way He said to do them. In that way, wholeness will come to all. Society may afflict, but the house of the Lord heals. Let those whose dignity has been battered by society find glory and honor in the Church!

10

Black Is Beautiful...
And So Is White

As I urged you when I went into Macedonia, stay
there in Ephesus so that you may command certain
men not to teach false doctrines any longer

Nor to devote themselves to myths and endless
genealogies. These promote controversies rather than
God's work — which is by faith.

1 Timothy 1:3,4

Have nothing to do with godless myths and old
wives' tales.

1 Timothy 4:7

One of the sad things that is happening in our
day is that ridiculous and outlandish teachings are
coming forth from some of the pulpits in America in an
attempt to restore dignity to black men and women. For
example, one such doctrine says that black people are
actually the lost tribe of Dan. To anyone who knows the
Bible, such a thought is absurd.

The point I want to make is, *we don't need myths and
fables to dignify black people*. There are many great black
men and women in the Bible. We will examine some of
them in this chapter.

We have already talked about the fact that Ham
and his sons, Cush, Mizraim, Put and Canaan, were

93

black. Ham, Cush, Mizraim and Put were never cursed!
The black people of this world were never told by God
that they were a cursed people, destined to lowly positions of servitude. It is now time to disclose the truth
and set people free.

Cush had a son named Nimrod. (Gen. 10:8-11.)
Since Cush was black, Nimrod was black as well. The
Bible says that Nimrod became a mighty warrior on the
earth and a mighty hunter before the Lord.

Nimrod grew to be a king and was the founder of
some of the world's most notorious kingdoms, Babylon
and Assyria being two of them. After the flood, black
people were the original settlers of the land between
the Tigris and Euphrates Rivers.

Nimrod was very resourceful and built entire
cities. Thus, we can say that the first great man and the
first king on the earth after the flood was a black man.
There is, however, great conflict over whether this black
man was "for the Lord" or "against the Lord." Nimrod's
name means "rebel,"[1] and the kingdoms he founded
became enemies of God and Israel.

Judah married a black Canaanite woman who bore
him three sons. (Gen. 38:2-5.)

Simeon had a black Canaanite wife and had a son
by her. (Gen. 46:10.)

Joseph married an African woman named Asenath.
(Gen. 41:45.) Melanin testing has proven that the
ancient Egyptians, including the Pharaohs, were black.
It is therefore quite safe to assume that Asenath was
black. Regardless of her shade, we know that she was a
descendant of a black man, Ham. Joseph and Asenath
had two sons, Ephraim and Manasseh. (Gen. 46:20.)
Their grandfather, Jacob, who later became Israel,

adopted these two dark-skinned boys as his very own sons, and they became two of the twelve tribes of Israel.

Through Ephraim and Manasseh, the black heritage of Ham flowed into the very nation of Israel by God's design and sovereign choosing. The names of Ephraim and Manasseh are mentioned 196 times in the Bible. Ephraim and Manasseh were descendants of Ham and had black African blood in their veins. Thus, all the Jewish descendants of Ephraim and Manasseh would be related to Ham, the black son of Noah.

Moses had a black wife. Numbers 12:1 KJV says, **And Miriam and Aaron spake against Moses because of the Ethiopian woman whom he had married: for he had married an Ethiopian woman.** *The New International Version* of the Bible calls Moses' wife a Cushite. This is proof positive that Cush, the black son of Ham, became the father of the Ethiopians. Moses and his black wife, Zipporah, had two sons, Gershom and Eliezer. (Ex. 18:3,4.)

Many believe that David's wife, Bathsheba, was black. The name *Bathsheba* means "daughter of Sheba." There are three Shebas in Scripture. One is the black grandson of Cush, one is a descendant of Shem (Gen. 10:22-28), the other is the grandson of Abraham and Keturah. (1 Chron. 1:32.) One is black and the others are Jewish.

A close study of the Hebrew language shows that Bathsheba was Jewish and not black. The black *Sheba* is pronounced "sheb-aw'."[2] The Jewish *Sheba* is pronounced "Sheh'-bah."[3] Bathsheba is "Bath-sheh'-bah" and is therefore the Jewish *Sheba*.[4]

There was a young black man in the army of Israel. He is mentioned in 2 Samuel 18:21-23. When Joab and his men were fighting Absalom, Joab sent a black man to give King David the good news of victory.

We know Solomon, the son of David, king of Israel, had an African wife. (1 Kings 3:1.) He talks about his black wife in The Song of Solomon. The love of Solomon's life says, **I am black, but comely** (Song of Sol. 1:5 KJV). *Comely* means beautiful! Thus, the Word of God says, "Black is beautiful!" The phrase, "Black is beautiful" did not originate in the 1960s. It is a truth from the Word of God. If God says, "Black is beautiful," then black *is* beautiful!

A powerful queen once heard of Solomon's wisdom and paid him a visit. This queen was very wealthy. She gave Solomon 4 1/2 tons of gold and many precious stones! We know her as the Queen of Sheba. She was black. The Hebrew word *Sheba* is the Ethiopian "Sheba" and not the Jewish "Sheba." King Solomon received her as royalty and gave her many gifts out of his royal bounty. (1 Kings 10:1-13.)

The Old Testament reveals that God sent the black king, Tirhakah, to distract and fight the king of Assyria, who had blasphemed God and was about to destroy Jerusalem. (2 Kings 19:9.) This black man saved Israel!

There is another black king mentioned in the Bible. Unfortunately, instead of saving Israel, he fought against Israel. His name was Zerah. His story is told in 2 Chronicles 14:9-14. Stories such as this prove that black people were not cursed and destined to be lowly slaves. The Bible portrays many blacks as wealthy kings and queens.

Two prophetic words about the black people of Africa appear in the book of Psalms. Psalm 68:31 says, **Cush will submit herself to God**. And Psalm 87:4 says, **I will record Rahab and Babylon among those who** acknowledge me — Philistia too, and Tyre, along with Cush — and will say, "This one was born in Zion."

The psalmist prophesied that the black people of Africa would be born again and have their names written in the Lamb's Book of Life!

A black man by the name of Ebed-Melech was an official in the royal palace during the days of Jeremiah, the prophet. He interceded with the king when Jeremiah was put into the cistern. (Jer. 38:7-13.) Because of this black official, Jeremiah was rescued and his life was saved. God honored this black man and gave Jeremiah a special prophecy for him.

> While Jeremiah had been confined in the courtyard of the guard, the word of the Lord came to him:
>
> "Go and tell Ebed-Melech the Cushite, 'This is what the Lord Almighty, the God of Israel, says: I am about to fulfill my words against this city through disaster, not prosperity. At that time they will be fulfilled before your eyes.
>
> But I will rescue you on that day, declares the Lord; you will not be handed over to those you fear.
>
> I will save you; you will not fall by the sword but will escape with your life, because you trust in me, declares the Lord'"
>
> **Jeremiah 39:15-18**

The prophet Zephaniah was a black man. Scripture says, **The word of the Lord that came to Zephaniah son of Cushi** (Zeph. 1:1). *Cushi* means a Cushite or descendant of Cush. It can also be translated "Ethiopian." The fact that Zephaniah was part African did not stop him from speaking out against black people who were at that time coming against Israel. (Zeph. 2:12.) This illustrates the point that we are related more through "grace" than through "race"! When you have to choose who you are identified with, you must choose the Lord, even if it means standing against others of your race! We don't take a stand based on race. We take a stand based on the truth of God's Word.

Let's look at the genealogy of Jesus. Both Matthew and Luke record the genealogy of Christ. In Matthew, five women are recorded as part of the lineage of Christ. They are Tamar, Rahab, Ruth, Bathsheba and Mary. Tamar, Bathsheba and Mary were of Jewish descent. Rahab and Ruth were Gentiles. The Lord Jesus had Jews and Gentiles in His genealogy. A Gentile was anyone who was non-Jewish.

All the descendants of the black Ham and the white Japheth were Gentiles. Jesus' heritage represents every color of man.

What about the Lord Jesus Himself? Jesus Christ of Nazareth was a Jew. He was not a European Caucasian, nor was He a black African. It is wrong for white people to characterize Jesus as a white man with blond hair and blue eyes. It is equally wrong for black people to depict Jesus as African.

No one has the right to change the Son of God. We must accept Him as He is. Jesus was a Jew. He looked like a Jew, born in Israel. The people of Israel have a dark olive complexion. He was the perfect blend between black and white. Jesus can relate to all men of every color.

In the New Testament, a certain Simon of Cyrene helped Jesus carry His cross. (Matt. 27:32.) Cyrene was located in northern Africa, near Libya. Thus, at the most pivotal moment in history, God had an African, a black man, on the scene to aid His Son. Think of the honor given to this black man. Only one person could carry the cross of Christ, and God in His sovereignty chose a black man for the job. Black people were carrying the cross of Christ long before they were bearing the crescent of Islam. Islam is not the religion of the black race, Christianity is!

In Acts 8, Philip, the evangelist, was supernaturally led to an Ethiopian eunuch, a black man. This Ethiopian was an important official in charge of all the treasury of Candace, queen of the Ethiopians. (Acts 8:26-38.) This black man was no slave. He was a high-ranking dignitary and administrator in charge of hugh sums of money. God loved him and led Philip to him so he could hear the message of Jesus and be saved. He became a believer and was baptized. In all of the New Testament, there is not another case where God so miraculously moved to reach one man.

The racial diversity of the church at Antioch is very exciting. Scripture says, **In the church at Antioch there were prophets and teachers: Barnabas, Simeon called Niger, Lucius of Cyrene, Manaen (who had been brought up with Herod the tetrarch) and Saul** (Acts 13:1). What a unique group of men!

Barnabas was of Jewish descent. Simeon, called Niger, was a black man. *Niger* means "black."[5] Lucius was a dark African from Cyrene. Manaen was a Gentile, the foster brother of Herod Antipas. Saul was Jewish.

In this group of men, we have two Jews, two Africans and one Greek. All of them were saved and filled with the Holy Spirit, and each held a five-fold ministry office. It is important to see that this was an ethnically mixed group of men who led the church at Antioch. Again, note that African people were committed to Christ and His Church long before they were committed to Islam!

There is plenty of truth in the Bible that dignifies black people. There is no need in resorting to myths or fables. The Word of God speaks well of all men.

The white descendants of Japheth are mentioned in the Bible as well. In Genesis 10:2, Javan, the son of Japheth, is mentioned. Josephus records that Javan became the father of all the Grecians. With this in mind, we will look at some references in the Bible concerning the Greek people or Hellenists.

In John 12:20,21, we are told that there were some Greeks (white descendants of Japheth) who went to worship God at the Jewish feast. They approached Philip with a request that has become very famous, **"Sir," they said, "we would like to see Jesus"** (v. 21).

Cornelius, an Italian, was a very devout believer in God. He served God to the best of his knowledge and sought the Lord with all of his heart. God rewarded this white man with an angelic visitation that resulted in the Apostle Peter being supernaturally summoned to his house to bring the Gospel message. This white man and his household accepted Christ. They were baptized in the Holy Spirit and in water. (Acts 10.)

As the Gospel began to spread, some men from Cyprus and Cyrene went to Antioch and preached the good news about Jesus to the Greeks. These men were some of the very first to ignore the racial barriers of their day. They stepped over the color line to tell these white people about Jesus. Many who heard the message believed. (Acts 11:20,21.)

Timothy, the young man who became closely associated with the Apostle Paul, was a white man. His mother was Jewish, but his father was a Greek. (Acts 16:1,3.) This white man became a great apostle and preacher of the Gospel and was Paul's right-hand man. He is mentioned in the New Testament twenty-four times. Two books in the Word of God are named after this youthful, light-skinned man.

In Thessalonica, Paul won a large number of Greeks to the Lord. (Acts 17:4.)

As Paul preached Jesus, many prominent Greek men and women were won to the Lord in Berea. (Acts 17:12.)

Paul's campaign to win the white descendants of Japheth to the Lord continued in Athens where he reasoned in the synagogue with Jews and God-fearing Greeks. (Acts 17:16,17.) Paul saturated the area with the Gospel so all the Jews and Greeks who lived in the province of Asia heard the word of the Lord. (Acts 19:10.)

In Galatians 2:3, we are told that another one of Paul's sons in the faith, Titus, was a white man. Titus is mentioned eleven times in the Bible, and a book in the New Testament bears his name.

Since Paul ministered in Asia Minor, many white people are mentioned in the New Testament. The Galatians were white descendants of Japheth and his son, Gomer.

The Bible is not a biased book. It shows plainly that God loves us all and wants all men to be saved.

When God crowned man with glory and honor (Ps. 8:4,5), He gave man His beauty. The glory of God is a beautiful thing. All men possess it, because each one has been created in the image of God. Therefore, we must conclude that black is beautiful...and so is white!

11

Don't Blame Us!

"Don't blame us" would be the message that many white people would convey to black people.

Many black people have the attitude that white people are to be personally blamed and held accountable for everything bad that has happened to them over the last 350 years. Should every white man, woman and child be held responsible for the plight of the African-Americans? Would it be right and just to say that every American Caucasian is at fault?

I look at my own family as an example. My family was not involved in any of the slave trading of the 1600s and 1700s. My relatives never owned a slave. In fact, Great-Grandpa Hellmann never arrived in America until 1882. That was seventeen years after the Civil War ended. When my great grandfather arrived from Germany, he was a poor common laborer. He worked in a soap factory in St. Louis, Missouri. He was a poor white immigrant. Is he to be blamed for enslaving black people?

The truth is, no white person alive today is directly responsible for what happened hundreds of years ago to the African people. Let's be honest. If we all lived back then, some would have become involved in buying, selling and owning slaves, but many would not! Are we guilty by association? Isn't that being prejudiced? How can we blame an entire race because of the acts of a few? How can we blame a generation who was not even alive when the atrocities took place?

If the white people of today are guilty for what some of our race did 350 years ago, does this mean that every African-American alive today is guilty for the enslavement of the Israelites? It was the descendants of Ham who enslaved Israel for 400 years and worked them ruthlessly. Are the present-day descendants of Ham still guilty? Of course not!

What about the German people? Is every German person alive today guilty of the holocaust? I'm of German descent on both my mother and father's side. Is God holding me responsible for the murder of six million Jews? Is the newest newborn baby in Berlin guilty of gassing Jewish boys and girls? No! If we are to continue in this erroneous thinking, we must at least be consistent. If all the white people of today are guilty of the original enslavement of Africans, then all of African descent are guilty for enslaving Israel. Furthermore, all Germans are guilty of murdering six million Jews.

The Word of God tells us that none of us are held accountable for the sins of someone else! We are not responsible for the sins of our forefathers. Each individual is accountable only for his own personal sin. He is not responsible for anyone else's. This matter is addressed in the book of Ezekiel, chapter 18:

> The word of the Lord came to me:
>
> "What do you people mean by quoting this proverb about the land of Israel: `The fathers eat sour grapes, and the children's teeth are set on edge'?
>
> "As surely as I live, declares the Sovereign Lord, you will no longer quote this proverb in Israel.

"For every living soul belongs to me, the father
as well as the son — both alike belong to me. *The soul
who sins is the one who will die.*"

Ezekiel 18:1-4

Ezekiel goes on to give examples of what he is talking about. The first illustration is about a righteous father who has a wicked son. Will the wicked son live because he had a righteous father? The Word of God says, **He will not!** (Ezek. 18:5-13.) What if there is a wicked father who has a righteous son? Will the righteous son die because of his father's sin? No! He will not die for his father's sin; he will surely live. But the father will die for his own sin. (Ezek. 18:14-18.) Listen carefully! **The soul who sins is the one who will die.** *The son will not share the guilt of the father*, **nor will the father share the guilt of the son. The righteousness of the righteous man will be credited to him, and the wickedness of the wicked will be charged against him** (v. 20).

Ezekiel is not the only book in Scripture where this truth is recorded. Deuteronomy 24:16 states plainly, **Fathers shall not be put to death for their children, nor children put to death for their fathers; each is to die for his own sin.**

King Amaziah followed this precept. After an assassination, King Amaziah put the assassins to death but let their sons live. (2 Kings 14:1-6.)

In the third commandment, God says He will punish or bless children for what their parents do. (Ex. 20:4-6.) Notice, this statement is not made in connection with every commandment but only the commandment concerning idolatry. The curse brought on by idolatry as well as the blessing brought on by love for God are passed down through many generations.

Perhaps it could be explained this way. If someone worships idols and hates the Lord, he is going to pass that idolatrous lifestyle and hatred for the Lord on to his children. They, too, will worship idols and hate God. They will likewise die as did their father. On the other hand, there are those who love the Lord. They will pass that love for God on to their children, who in turn will pass it on to still another generation. Love for God or hatred for God can be passed from one generation to another.

Ezekiel makes it plain that anyone can break out of this cycle. If your father loved God but you are an infidel, you are going to hell. Your father's love for God cannot save you. If your father is the infidel and you love the Lord, you are not going to hell because of your father! His unbelief cannot condemn you. Every person in hell is there because of *his own sins*.

Paul said, **So then, each of us will give an account of himself to God** (Rom. 14:12). We will not have to give an account for the things our forefathers have done. Each must face Jesus Christ and answer for his own life!

Therefore, according to Scripture, you cannot blame the white people of today for enslaving black people 350 years ago. Those who did that crime will have to answer for themselves before the Lord.

As we stated in a previous chapter, through the tool of the Civil War, God judged this country for the initial enslavement of the African people. Notice, the generation God judged was the generation that actually owned slaves and perpetuated slavery.

Now, let's take another look at our "don't blame us" axiom. Let's look at it from another point of view.

Can the white people of today be rightly blamed for the present situation of some African-Americans?

Until a few years ago, black Americans were not permitted to go to public schools or universities. They were not allowed to vote. There were many things they were not allowed to do. Who was it that would not allow them to do these things? We must answer truthfully, the white establishment. White people have been in control of this country since its inception. We have been in control politically, economically, educationally, socially and racially.

What happens to a people who are not allowed to get an education? Usually, those who are best educated rise to the top of a society. The poorly educated sink to the bottom. Lack of knowledge is a destroyer of men. (Hos. 4:6.) By depriving black Americans of a first-class education, we pushed them to the bottom rung on the social and economic ladder. People who are not allowed an education are destined for a life of poverty, and poverty breeds crime. When is the last time you heard about a rich person robbing a 7-Eleven Store? Have you ever heard of doctors, lawyers, engineers, school teachers and business owners rumbling in the streets in gang warfare? Have you ever seen judges and bankers looting stores in the wave of riots or a natural disaster?

Of course, just because you are poor doesn't mean that you have to murder someone or become a criminal. Abraham Lincoln was poor, but he rose to become president of the United States. He was also white. A white society allowed white people, even the poor, to better themselves.

Only at this moment in American history are black Americans beginning to rise to their rightful place among men. More and more black Americans are being elected to public office and assuming judgeships, but it has taken two hundred years for these things to happen. We have not had a black president or vice-president. Rarely do we have black Santa Clauses. However, we have made progress. Look back thirty short years. In the 1960s, who would have thought that Birmingham and Atlanta would ever have black mayors? We've come a long way, but we have not arrived.

Can the white people of today be blamed for these things? Unfortunately, yes. White people have been the ones in control. When a white government, representing white people, will not let black people get an education, they are to be blamed for the ensuing poverty and social conditions.

On the other hand, not every white American has been part of the so-called establishment. As far back as the early 1700s, there were white people who vigorously opposed slavery. There were whites who aided black slaves in the 1800s and brought them to freedom. In 1909, white people were instrumental in the formation of the National Association for the Advancement of Colored People (NAACP).[1]

While guilt by association would be understandable, it still would not be absolutely correct.

Racism should no longer be used as an excuse for living in poverty. While there is still plenty of prejudice, we do live in a day when a good education is available to everyone. Housing is improving. When people are allowed to get an education, they get better-paying jobs. Better-paying jobs bring a higher standard of living. Anyone who really wants to learn can excel today. Anyone wishing to improve himself can do so. Anyone who wants to work hard can make it. That could not be said a few short years ago.

With the changes that are taking place, it is no longer acceptable to blame the white establishment.

However, there are still changes that need to be made. In some situations, black people are still turned down for jobs for which they are qualified. Some mortgage loans are denied that should be approved. In some situations, black people are fired from jobs unfairly. There are many racial injustices still taking place in our society. Not everyone is treated fairly in the United States of America.

The old way of thinking is not dead in everyone's mind. I live in a relatively new neighborhood. Our contractor had a large sign at the entrance of the subdivision that said, "Highly restricted neighborhood." Now, anyone with a brain knows what that means. It means that every house has to have so many square feet. It means that there are rules that govern the neighborhood to keep it clean. For example, you can't park cars on the street. All vehicles must be in the driveway. You can't put a motor home in your sideyard. Burning trash in the backyard is unacceptable. But there were actually some white people who came to buy houses because they thought it meant, "No blacks allowed." Unbelievable! With God's help, we can move on to better days where **brothers** [and sisters in Christ] **live together in unity!** (Ps. 133:1).

12

The Story of a Multicultural Church

After missing the will of God in a geographical move, my family and I returned to Huntsville, Alabama, June 30, 1983. We were excited, because a new chapter in our lives was about to begin. We were starting a new church the following Sunday, July 3. In my zeal to start the church, I did not take into consideration that it was the fourth of July week-end when many people would be out of town.

When Sunday arrived, we headed for the rundown motel room we had rented for our church meeting. To my utter amazement, there were forty-three men, women and children that first Sunday. Half of them I had known previously, but the other half were people I had never met. The entire congregation was white. They were a special group of people and are still very dear to us.

We met in a home for our first mid-week service. The congregation decided right then and there that we wanted to be a church that accepted all people. This ministry philosophy has stayed with us through the years. We have never strayed from that vision.

Within ten months, our church had grown to approximately ninety-five people. When a church facility became available in the north part of town, we jumped at the chance to buy it. We not only wanted our own building, but we wanted to be in the north part of town because it had racial diversity. We purposed to be a multicultural church. Even though our charter members were white, being multicultural was our goal.

Since there was not a solidly mixed congregation in our city, being truly interracial presented a challenge. Our city was comprised mainly of black churches and white churches. Some white churches had a few black members, but not many. I do not call a church a real multicultural church until there are black members who equally participate in the ministry of the church.

As we settled into our new location, it was about a year before a black person visited us. We did not do anything special, except we promised to love everyone and treat people with equality. This was not a show with us. We had the burden for racial blend and endeavored to live it. As a result, more and more black brothers and sisters began to come, and some joined the church.

It was a wonderful day and a great thing for the church when black people began to come and join Word of Truth. I am thankful to all of the black members of my church for giving me, a white man, the opportunity to be their pastor. It is truly a privilege. I am equally proud of the white members of Word of Truth, who desire to be multicultural and sincerely love people.

My congregation is now comprised of people who are as intense about being multiracial as I am. In fact, black and white alike, we are all passionate about it. We are all God's people, and we should be together. We have the very same Lord and the very same Spirit. We are saved by the very same blood and believe in the very same Scriptures. There are far more reasons to be together than to be apart. Besides, we need each other. White believers need black believers, and the black believers need the white believers.

I have pastored an all-white church, and I have pastored Word of Truth. From experience, I would say that no church can become all that God wants it to be until we have people of diversity in it. Different races of people bring different strengths and gifts into the Body. It is enriching to learn from other cultures.

Over the years, our church continued to grow. In 1992, almost two hundred people joined, and three-fourths of them were black. Soon Word of Truth had three hundred white members and three hundred black members. This was the work of God. Man did not do it. I did not do it. The Holy Spirit was building His church the way He wanted it to be.

Our racial problems have been few and minor. I will attempt to share with you some of these problems to help you avoid conflicts in the Body where you belong.

Since Word of Truth started as a white church, we had all white music. We had white musicians, singers and leaders. We also had white rhythm and style. The black members who came to this style of music were very kind and gracious. Never once, over a period of years, did I hear a complaint. As more and more black brothers and sisters joined, they became involved in all areas of ministry, including music.

At Word of Truth the doors of ministry and service are open to all. Soon, a dream was fulfilled, and we were able to put a predominately black choir on the stage to lead our praise services. Actually, we did not intend to have a black choir. The word went out that we were starting a choir, and the black members were the ones who responded to the call. The choir, led by a white brother, worked hard to please the Lord. They did an outstanding job, but problems arose. Until this time, we had all white musicians and singers. Now we had black instrumentalists and vocalists with their rhythm and style. It was awesome, but prejudice arose among a few.

When prejudice rears its ugly head, black people feel it. They have been so accustomed to it that they know when it is present. As our black members began to feel the prejudice, they began to respond with suspicion, doubt and distrust. The combination of prejudice and distrust produced an undercurrent that lasted for a while. The Holy Spirit is very sensitive, and He does not like undercurrents. They are divisive and hinder the flow of the Spirit. When an undercurrent is present, usually the church is in for some trouble.

One of my black members came to me on a Sunday morning and said, "When more black people come to our church, are you going to leave?" It was a fair but sad question. Black people are accustomed to white people leaving them. They know that whites talk about not being prejudiced, but their actions do not support their claims.

Another black lady came to me and said, "All we want is to live in peace. Why do white people not like us?"

Rejection is a terrible pill to swallow. It hurts to be rejected, especially if you are repeatedly rejected. I know. As a pastor, I have been rejected many times, by many people. As these two wonderful ladies spoke to me, I could feel their hurt. People should not be rejected and hurt in the house of the Lord.

I know good people, black and white. I can't understand what possible difference it makes that we are different colors. Why would anyone want to get away from someone who is a wonderful person? Prejudice doesn't make sense!

Our music was what Satan used to arouse the latent prejudice in some of our members. Every time people came to church and saw the predominately black choir, they were confronted with their own secret bigotry. White members began to leave the church for all kinds of reasons. They didn't like our music. We were not family-oriented. We were not as prophetic as we should be. They didn't like our Christian Academy. They didn't like us performing interracial marriages. All of the people who left were white, and they resettled in all-white churches. Of course, those who left never said they were prejudiced, but God knows the truth. During this same time, no black members left.

Another situation that may arise in a multicultural church is the lack of involvement by many of the white members. Usually black people are very zealous for the Lord and the church. If I asked for ten Sunday school teachers, more than ten black hands would go up. Very few, if any, white hands would be raised. If I needed ushers, greeters, soulwinners, nursery workers or ministers of any kind, the same would be true.

Because of this, it began to seem that the black brethren were doing everything. If a white person was listening to the devil, he or she might hear him say, "The blacks are taking over the church." They are not taking over the church. The white people simply were not volunteering for anything. If you sit down and do not participate, you have no one to blame but yourself. Thank God there are people who will get up and do the job. I could care less what color the people are who are doing the work of the ministry.

Blacks "taking over" is a hidden fear of carnally minded white people. My white brother and sister, get off your pew and become actively involved in the ministry of your church. Your apathy and non-involvement is what makes it appear that black brothers and sisters are "taking over the church." This fault does not belong to the black brethren; it clearly belongs to the white.

Let's be interested in Christ, not color! Concern yourself with the will of God, not the color of man. Quit accusing black people of wanting to take over.

Another obstacle is the racial paranoia of many black people. While I understand how this paranoia came to be and why it is there, it still can make things difficult. Some blacks can be ultra-sensitive and suspicious. They sense things that do not exist, and they interpret things wrongly. Because of the past, Satan lies to black people. If they are listening to his voice, they will hear him say, "There is a hidden agenda." Some black people think that there is always a hidden racial conspiracy among white people. This is not true.

In April of 1994, we started a congregation in the south part of our city. My thought was that we could reach new people who would not drive the distance to our church. I really did not consider that the south part of town was predominately white or that most black people do not feel wanted or comfortable in that part of town. This, in itself, is something we must change. Black people should be able to go wherever they want to go and live wherever they want to live. Those types of racial territorial spirits must be broken off our cities. Some of my black members thought that this was a move to start a white church. Nothing could have been further from my mind. Even so, Jesus said it was the sick who needed a physician. Those who are racially prejudiced are sick, sin sick. That is all the more reason for us to be in the south part of town. If no one challenges the territorial spirits, they will continue to reign.

Racial paranoia causes people to hear things through racial hearing aids and see things through racial glasses. In Christ, we take off the racial glasses of the natural man and receive the new vision of the Spirit. Therefore, church decisions should not be interpreted racially, but spiritually.

Jesus commanded us to love one another. White people are not just to love whites and black people are not just to love blacks. Love steps across the color line. We are commanded to love one another. As a Christian, you cannot be selective about the people you love and accept. The Bible says, **Accept one another, then, just as Christ accepted you, in order to bring praise to God** (Rom. 15:7).

Have a heart for people, and open your church to all races. You will be richer culturally and spiritually because of it.

13

Racial Etiquette

As God moves local churches to become multicultural, it is certain that there will be some "people wrecks." Collisions occur when two or more individuals bump into each other. They may offend one another, misunderstand each other or have a conflict over some issue.

People everywhere have conflicts and differences of opinion. Black people and white people are certain to collide as they attempt to relate to one another. This colliding is not bad. In fact, it is very good. If people were not getting close, there would be no collisions. The very fact that there are some collisions is a sign that people are attempting to relate. Don't fear these "accidents." They can actually be very positive! White people and black people have rarely been close, but God is changing that in His house. It is God's will that redeemed white people and redeemed black people be close, that they genuinely love one another, serve one another and walk in complete unity.

There are certain things that we must learn about each other. Sometimes we don't know what to say to one another. We are ignorant as to what offends. The purpose of this chapter is to give some basic helps for successful multicultural relationships.

Love is the key. Jesus has given His people a serious command. We have all been commanded by the

Lord Jesus to love one another. (John 13:34,35.) This is not a command for all white people to love white people and all black people to love black people. This command is for all people to love all people. We are not given the freedom by Jesus to pick and choose the people we will love.

If you are a Christian, you are commanded to love people of all races! You don't have a choice in the matter. People of the world are not going to love anyone but themselves. However, we are not the people of the world. We are the people of God. As the people of God, we are commanded to love all the other people of God, regardless of race, nationality or ethnic background. The love of Christ transcends all barriers.

When you attend a multicultural church, you can be assured that the people there are serious about love. After all, there are many segregated churches. You could easily go to one or the other. But to purposely go to a church that is interracial shows that you are serious about love.

As people attempt to come together, we must realize that most white people have never had a close personal friend who is black. I suspect that most black people have never had a close personal friend who is white. That means this is new territory for all of us. We are pioneers blazing a trail of love, acceptance and forgiveness. We are daring to go where no man has gone before. We dare to cross racial bridges and climb racial mountains that people have been afraid of for centuries. God has always used pioneers to accomplish His purposes and bring multitudes into a new movement of the Spirit.

The history of the modern Church, beginning with Martin Luther, is the story of God raising up men and women who were supernaturally called, anointed and sent to restore truth to the Body of Christ. How exciting to be on the cutting edge of the Spirit. God intends to bring black people and white people together as one in Christ! Should Jesus tarry, the years ahead will see the breakdown of all racial barriers in the Church. Of course, there are churches where no one is really saved, including the preacher. They are social and political churches that have no life. These churches will not change. The true Church of the living God is going to change and change racially!

Because we have had few friends of another race or culture, we have rarely interacted with one another. Sometimes problems arise from our ignorance and inexperience.

First, we must understand that American society has been dominated by the white race. The white race has been on top and the black race on the bottom. This causes two problems. The first is that white people look down on black people. This positioning of whites on top and blacks on the bottom is not only a positioning in our society, but it is also a positioning in our minds! White people see themselves as better than black people. However, the closer you get to Jesus, the more He is going to take this spirit and error out of you. White people are not better than black people. The very thought is sin!

Our minds have been programmed by a racially prejudiced world. If you are a Christian, you are not supposed to be in the "white mind." You're supposed to be in your "right mind." You are to possess a "new" or "renewed mind" and have the "mind of Christ." This white mentality also causes white people to talk down to black people. Many don't mean to. It is just the way our society has been programmed. White people speak from an "on top" position. It comes across, not only in what we say, but in how we say it.

A white person in the church may say to a black person, "We are so glad you are joining us." We, who? We white people. The statement could be construed to mean, "We white people are so glad to have you black people join us white people." If we are not careful, we may tend to position ourselves on top when talking to a black person. If you're white, you don't think any- thing of it. If you're black, you get tired of being put in a subordinate position, even in everyday conversation. There is a better way to say things! Why not say, "I am so glad to see white people and black people coming together in Christ"? That statement positions no one on top or bottom but is a statement of equality.

Notice, the dividing line is in the use of our pro- nouns, "we - you," "us - them." The moment you use the words "we" and "you," "us" and "them," you have just divided the Church. In a multicultural church, we and us should refer to everyone in the church. If it refers to a specific group of people in the Church, you have divided the Body. Watch carefully how you use pronouns, for they can be divisive!

Things also slip out of our mouths that show how racially indoctrinated we have become. Three or four years ago, I was home recovering from an illness. As I flipped through the television channels, I noticed the Oprah Winfrey show was on. On this particular day, she was doing her show from a county in Georgia, noted for its racial prejudice. Her whole show was about prejudice.

There were all kinds of people in the crowd. There were people who were against racial prejudice, and

and there were bikers with leather jackets bearing the Confederate flag. The conversation was hot and heavy.

Suddenly, a little white Georgia housewife had something to say. She was angry with prejudice and didn't want any more of it in her county. She was speaking up for black people and addressing her remarks mainly to the old south rebels in the crowd. My eyes were glued to the TV. This young white woman was going to set things straight. She got the microphone.

The word *nigger* had been brought up in the program, and this lady was furious. She said, "The word nigger has nothing to do with the color of one's skin. It has to do with the kind of person you are. There are white 'niggers' and black 'niggers.'" She raised her hand and pointed straight at the rebel, flag-bearing bikers.

She proceeded, "If the truth be known, there are niggers in this room right now." This little lady was calling these white bikers "niggers." I couldn't believe what I was hearing. What boldness and courage. But, wait a minute! What was the rest of her statement? "If the truth be known, there are niggers in this room right now (pause) *besides Oprah*!"I could not believe my ears. She just called Oprah a nigger on nationwide television. Oprah's mouth dropped open.

The woman suddenly realized what she had said. Flushed with embarrassment, she said, "I didn't mean you are a nigger, Oprah." This lady had meant well. She was passionate about ending racial prejudice. She felt strongly about it. But all of a sudden, society spoke right through her mouth. The Holy Spirit is getting carnal society out of us and putting the Kingdom of God within.

If you are black, you could say, "All white people are just alike. They'll never change. There is no hope."

But I disagree. This little white Georgia housewife was changing! She had not arrived yet, but her journey was well underway.

People who really follow Jesus are changing. None of us, black or white, have arrived. Now is not the time to throw up your hands in disgust. It is time to learn, ask for forgiveness and go forward.

A second problem caused by the white on top, black on bottom model, is this; while white people naturally speak from an "on top" position, black people hear and speak from a "defensive" position. Blacks are accustomed to having to defend themselves. This can make relating to black people a difficult thing.

Defensiveness clouds our hearing and understanding. It causes you to hear things incorrectly. You hear racial bias where there is none. You completely misunderstand what is said and totally take things the wrong way. Defensiveness will cause you to stay offended most of the time. You can always find something wrong. It's not hard. Defensive people do not get along well with others. Just as white people have things to learn and overcome in order to properly relate, so do black people. Because of this defensiveness, white people could say, "I'm afraid to talk. I'm afraid to say anything."

It's best not to be so sensitive. While people may love you, they will start avoiding you because sensitive people always take things the wrong way. Then feelings get hurt and tempers flair. It is most unpleasant. Pretty soon people will just stop trying to relate to you, because relating to you has been such a painful experience in the past.

Some of the black brothers and sisters are extremely sensitive, and some are not sensitive at all. This is most confusing to the white brethren who don't know whether to talk to you or leave you alone. If they are leaving you alone, it may not be because they are prejudiced but because they don't know what to do, given your sensitivity and defensiveness. Simply put, it is no fun being around sensitive and defensive people. No one likes walking on eggshells. It would do well to commit to memory 1 Corinthians 13:4-8 as a means of renewing our minds. At the heart of this Scripture is, "Love is not touchy (defensive). It is not easily angered, and it rejoices when truth is revealed."

As we relate, it is imperative that we look at the heart and intent of the speaker. If something is misstated, was it said with malicious intent or innocently spoken? There is a big difference. We have to give each other the space and opportunity to grow.

Let mistakes be an occasion to learn. I am open to learning. I have told my whole congregation, "If I misstate something, don't get angry with me and call me prejudiced. Come to me and teach me a better way of saying things." We will not learn unless we are taught. We need knowledge, not fear, defensiveness and the resulting polarization.

For black people and white people to relate, we also must understand that each has had their own negative experiences with those of the opposite race. The negative experiences of the past must be overcome. Most white people have no understanding or comprehension of the things black people have been through. If we could only walk in one another's shoes, how helpful it would be.

On the other hand, some black people are unaware that there are white people who have been persecuted by black people. Let me give you an example. I know a young white couple who, while attending school, were tyrannized by some of the black students. This wife had terrible memories of black boys pawing her body. It was humiliating and embarrassing. On one occasion, she was punched in the face. The husband had experiences in school where black boys surrounded him, beat him up and took his lunch money. This type of harassment has happened.

As we relate to each other, there are past experiences that must be overcome. In the case of this white couple, they were overcoming with the help of the Lord. They held no grudge against black people because of what had happened to them. We need not hold everyone who is white or black guilty because of a few. It is unfair and unjust to lump everyone together.

People of this world purposely talk in divisive ways. A news broadcast may say that a white police officer shot a black man, or a black police officer shot a white man. What does black and white have to do with it? Why can't we say a police office shot a man?

Satan makes sure that we label everyone white or black. He knows what he is doing. By putting a color on everyone, he brings division and antagonism. It is important to Satan and his purposes that everyone's color be mentioned. By saying that a white police officer shot a black man, we are subtly suggesting that the white man shot the black man because he was black. Or the black police officer shot the white man for revenge. Isn't that what is implied? We're not naive enough to say that such things have never happened, but we also know that the media talks this way to make everything that happens a racial issue.

Racial issues have been made out of things that were never racial to begin with. Why can't we talk about each other as people instead of colors? Have you ever noticed when a white police officer shoots a white man, it is not reported in racial terms of what color each was? When dissimilar, a person's color makes better copy. The press can get more mileage out of it. It makes better reading and sells more newspapers.

The love of money is at the very core of such willful racial antagonism. While people get inflamed reading or listening to such reporting, there are those who are laughing all the way to the bank. Lost humanity does not care who gets hurt as long as there is money to be made. Let's wise up!

14
Destroying Racial Barriers: A Synopsis

Here are thirteen key principles for destroying racial barriers, summarizing the teaching in this book:

1. *God is the One Who is going to have to break all racial barriers.* Man has failed miserably in this arena, and only God can do what man cannot do. Just as the anointing destroys the yoke (Isa. 10:27 KJV), the anointing is going to destroy prejudice, segregation, superiority, inferiority, delusion and pride. God is going to use chosen servants, black and white, to herald this move of God, which is already well underway in the land. Racial barriers will indeed be destroyed in the Body of Christ, but not by might or power, only by the working of the Spirit of the Lord. The Spirit of the Lord will succeed where man has failed. It's going to be exciting and supernatural.

This destruction of racial barriers is itself going to bring revival! Many have prayed for revival, and it's just like God to send it in a way that is totally unexpected. Prepare yourself to meet this new move of God! *Racial barriers can only be destroyed by the Holy Spirit!*

2. *A change of mind, thought, philosophy and perspective is a must to move on with God.* We have all been so immersed and entrenched in our "own way of think-

ing" that we need to be blasted out of our mental ruts! Neither black people nor white people have been totally correct in the way they think or in the way they see things.

Quit holding on to black pride and white pride, and be transformed by the renewing of your mind. We must think like God. The traditional perspectives of man must go. To break down racial barriers, we must all start seeing ourselves and our past from God's perspective. We have all sinned and fallen short of the glory of God. For over three hundred years, black people and white people have been blaming each other. It has gotten us nowhere. It is time for whites and blacks to accept responsibility and change.

Be truthful with yourself about yourself and your race. No race is made up of angels. One race is just as sinful as another. *Racial barriers can only be destroyed when we see things from God's perspective instead of man's!*

3. *Sin is the problem on this earth.* Sin is in all of us and has been from the beginning. The problem is not that we are all different colors. The problem is not even that we have different cultures. The problem is that we are all sinful.

Sinful people do not treat each other right. We should have learned that the moment Cain murdered Abel. Not only do we not treat those of another race right, we don't even treat those of our own race right. Whites fight whites. Blacks fight blacks. Superiority and inferiority are not just arguments among the races, they are arguments within the races. The demonized Adolf Hitler did not say that Caucasians were superior. He said only German Caucasians were superior. To Hitler, Caucasians were not the master race, the Germans were.

Even within the races, superiority and inferiority are issues.

Because we are all sinful, God has from time to time sent certain judgments on us all. Centuries ago, Jerusalem was destroyed and the people of Israel were taken into captivity by the Babylonians. Five hundred years ago, the lands of the Native Americans were taken from them and given to another nation. Three hundred years ago, the black man of Africa was removed to a foreign land. One hundred and thirty years ago, white America was judged with the bloodiest, most destructive and costliest war in her history. A few short years ago, God used America to discipline Iraq and Saddam Hussein. Most, if not all, of the nations and peoples of this world have at one time been disciplined by the sovereign, all-powerful God of heaven. Let's quit making every issue a racial issue. Sin, not skin, is the real problem in this world. *Racial barriers can only be destroyed when we understand that race is not the problem, sin is.*

4. *God can take anything bad and turn it into good!* This is exactly what He did in the life of Joseph. Joseph became a common slave in Egypt. He was taken into slavery against his will. He was sold for money. He was transported to a foreign land. Mistreated, imprisoned and shackled, he saw the hand of God in his life working redemption. He refused to be bitter, angry and vengeful.

All who have been likewise mistreated can see God bringing good out of bad and can choose to be "better" rather than "bitter." The choice is up to you. Joseph told his brothers not to worry about what they had done to him because it was God Who had sent him ahead to save their lives. Joseph had a positive perspective. You can choose to see God or man. You can choose better over bitter and positive over negative.

The choices you make will be the ones you live with the rest of your life. They will also determine the attitudes you pass on to your children. *Racial barriers can only be destroyed when we see God at work instead of man.*

5. *We may have different colors of skin, but we are all one blood and related through our common ancestor, Noah.* Through Noah and his wife, the different races of men came into being. Noah had three sons, each one of a different color. Ham was the black son of Noah, Shem the olive-complected son and Japheth the white son.

Scientifically, this is possible, if Noah and his wife were dark. Biblically, this is possible because God is the Creator of all men and designed and created us just as He wanted us to be.

All men have been created in the image and likeness of God. If all bear His image, then all were created equal. No race of men was created to be superior or inferior, and all were created with equal intelligence.

After the flood, the black Ham sinned, and Noah cursed Ham's son, Canaan. The curse was not put on Ham or on Ham's other black sons — Cush, Mizraim and Put. Since the Canaanites were cursed, God, in time, took their land and gave it to Abraham, Isaac and Jacob.

Cush is the founder of the Ethiopian people. Mizraim founded Egypt and Put is the progenitor of Libya, in northern Africa. Thus, the black people of Africa were never cursed! *Racial barriers can only be destroyed when we realize that no race is cursed. All races came from God through Noah!*

6. *Prejudice is a sin, and as Christians, we are not allowed to have it in our lives.* Neither are we allowed to have hostility or anger in our hearts toward any person

or race of people. Hostility, hatred and anger are from the flesh and not from the Spirit of God.

While people of the world are obviously controlled by the flesh, we who are Christians are to be controlled by the Spirit. True Christians don't hate people or races of people. If there is hatred or animosity in your heart toward white people or black people, get rid of it. Don't excuse it, nurse it or feed it. Repent of it. Even the Apostle Peter had deep prejudice in his heart, and God had to supernaturally deliver him.

All people are not alike. It is a grave mistake to lump all white people or all black people together and judge all on the merits and conduct of a few. We learned most of our prejudice from other people, generally relatives.

As Christians, it is time to go to the Word of God and replace the damaging, negative teaching of parents, grandparents, teachers, preachers and friends with love and truth.

Classes of people are not to be confused with races of people. There are low-class people in this world, and they come in all colors. But Christ loves them and wishes to lift them up. *Racial barriers can only be destroyed when we acknowledge that prejudice is sin.*

7. *Jesus Christ came and offered us new birth.* This new birth puts us in a new family, the family of God. When one enters the family of God, he is spiritually related to all other believers all over the world. It is called in Scripture, "the brotherhood of believers." We are no longer part of a white brotherhood or a black brotherhood. In fact, we are no longer related to all white people or all black people. We are only related to others who have experienced this new birth as we have.

We are now related through Spirit, not skin; through grace, not race; through character, not color! "Our people" are not other white people or other black people. "Our people" are now all saved people. Saved people are "my people." If you're not saved, you're not one of "my people." God has not authorized a white brotherhood or a black brotherhood, only a born-again brotherhood made up of blood-washed, Spirit-filled, overcoming children of God.

When we came to Christ, we lost worldly identities and Christ became our new identity. Our new identity is no longer white or black, it is Christian. We also lost the worldly "causes" of the natural man. Ministering Christ to every creature is our new cause. It is the cause of the black believer and the white believer. *Racial barriers can only be destroyed when we realize that Christ has made black believers and white believers, brothers.*

8. *God is a God of variety.* He has made us different. Everyone does not have to be like you. No man is the measuring rod by which all others are to be judged. God is the measuring rod. Just because someone is different doesn't mean they are better or worse than you. We are different, but equal. Why is it that we are threatened by someone who is different? Why do we fear someone who is different? Man has many insecurities that must be overcome. *Racial barriers can only be destroyed when we realize that variety is of God.*

9. *Dignity! We all need it.* Deep in the heart of man is the thirst for dignity, self-respect and self-esteem. It is an important part of our makeup. All people need to feel good about themselves. When man is habitually put down, a volcano erupts within. That volcano is the image of God. This is exactly what triggered the Civil Rights Movement of the 1960s. The image of God in black people exploded and said, "Enough is enough! We are as valuable as anyone else. Since God made us

all and since all were created in His image and in His likeness, all were created with an innate dignity and self-esteem." Feeling good about yourself starts when you know that you have been made to be like God.

How demoralizing is the doctrine of evolution which says we are like animals. Humanism tries to correct this by saying that we are gods. Both evolution and humanism are miserable failures in comparison to the truth of the Word of God.

No wonder Jesus said that we would know the truth and the truth would set us free. God has even made special provision in the Church to correct the lack of dignity and self-esteem that some bear. In the Church, special honor is to be given those who lacked it in the world. God wants you to have the dignity He created you to possess. When Satan stole man's dignity, he stole something that man cannot live without. The absence of dignity produces inferiority, fear, failure, pessimism, crime and poverty. Take a person's dignity from him and you ruin his whole life. Racial barriers can only be destroyed when we feel good about ourselves and when we feel good about others!

10. *The Word of God has many great things to say about black people.* There are many black people in the Bible. These black people are not ignorant, poor slaves. They are kings, queens and prophets. Many are pictured as being very wealthy. Many leading Bible characters had black wives. Among them are Judah, Simeon, Joseph and Moses. The greatest honor in the history of man was given to a dark African man, who helped Jesus carry His cross. Black Africans were serving the Lord Jesus long before the Islamic religion came into existence. *Racial barriers can only be destroyed when we see that black people are highly spoken of in the Word of God!*

11. *The white people of today are not to be blamed for the enslavement of the African people hundreds of years ago.* Each person will be judged for his own sins, not the sins of his father. If white people can still be blamed for the enslavement of black people, then black people can still be blamed for the enslavement of Joseph and Israel.

Certain white people can be blamed for the ongoing prejudice and injustice against black people. There is much prejudice in this world. We are nowhere near being rid of it. Black people are still being discriminated against. Most white people don't realize it, since they are not on the receiving end of such prejudice. *Racial barriers can only be destroyed when we forgive people and stop holding them responsible for the sins of their forefathers.*

12. *As churches become multicultural, clashes are bound to happen.* These clashes are often more positive than negative. Interracial churches are serious about love.

The two major problems facing such a church are the non-involvement of many white people and the paranoia of many black people. When black brothers and sisters come forward to serve the Lord and their church, many white people will say, "The blacks are taking over our church." The black brethren are not taking over, the white brethren are just not doing anything. This gives the church the appearance of being more black than white.

Black brethren, because they have been put down for so long, will be tempted to see and interpret everything in the church racially, instead of spiritually. Because of this, division will be perceived where there is none. *Racial barriers can only be destroyed when we walk in love!*

13. *In the Church, we must learn how to treat one another.* Most white people have never had a close black

friend, and most black people have never had a close white friend. There are things to learn!

White people generally talk down to black people, and black people can be very defensive. These two attitudes can make friendship and closeness a real problem. Pronouns can be very divisive. Watch carefully how you use "we," "you," "us," "them," and "they." These pronouns divide a congregation up into segments. "We" and "us" should refer to everyone in the local church. *Racial barriers can only be destroyed when we learn to be friends!*

God is preparing His Church for the greatest move since the beginning of mankind. Racial unity is the key that will unlock the door to revival. We must learn these simple steps to wholeness in our racial attitudes. We are about to experience an exciting new wave of God's glory and power. Our love for one another and unity in the Body of Christ will usher in our glorious King!

Endnotes

Chapter 2:

[1] *Grolier Electronic Publishing*. Release 6. Grolier, Inc., 1993. On line Computer Systems, Inc., 1987-1993. The Software Toolworks, Inc., 1993.

[2] Thayer, Joseph, D. D. *Thayer's Greek English Lexicon*. Grand Rapids, MI: Baker Book House, 1977, #'s 3340 & 3341, p. 405.

Chapter 3:

[1] Jones, Alfred. *Jones' Dictionary of Old Testament Proper Names*. Grand Rapids, MI: Kragel Publications, 1990, #3568, p. 89.

[2] *Ibid.*, #4714, p. 255.

[3] Whitaker, Charles. "Who Was Malcolm X?" *Ebony Magazine*, Johnson Publishing Co., pp. 120-125.

[4] Stump, Keith W. *The Middle East in Prophecy, Focus of End Time Events*, 1988 Worldwide Church of God, pp. 7,8.

[5] Halasa, Malu. *Elijah Muhammad*, New York & Philadelphia: Chelsea House Publishers, pp. 13,44,45,47.

[6] McKissic, Sr., William Dwight. *Beyond Roots: In Search of Blacks in the Bible*. Renaissance Productions, 1990, pp. 32,33.

[7] Dake, Finis Jennings. *Dake's Annotated Bible*. Atlanta, GA: Dake Bible Sales, 1963, Note "N," p. 9.

[8] Strong, James. *Strong's Concordance*. Hebrew-Chaldee Dictionary, 1890, #1368, p. 25.

[9] *Op. Cit., Grolier's Electronic Publishing*.

[10] Conniff, Michael L. & Davis, Thomas J. *Africans in the Americas*, New York: St. Martin's Press, pp. 41,42.

[11] *Op. Cit., Grolier's Electronic Publishing*.

Chapter 5:

[1] *Op. Cit.,* Strong, James, #3335, p. 51

[2] *Gesenius Hebrew-Chaldee Lexicon of the Old Testament.* Grand Rapids, MI: Baker Book House, 1979, #6083, p. 645.

[3] *Op. Cit.,* Jones, Alfred, #120, p. 12.

[4] *Ibid.,* "Noah," #5146, p. 280; "Shem," #8037, p. 329; "Ham," #2526, p. 138; "Japheth," #3315, p. 176.

[5] *Ibid.,* #2526, p. 138.

[6] *Ibid.,* "Cush," #3568, p. 89; "Mizraim," #4714, p. 255; "Put," #3166, p. 302; "Canaan," #3667, p. 81.

[7] *Ibid.,* #1586, p. 132.

[8] *Ibid.,* #4031, pp. 232,233.

[9] *Ibid.,* #4074, p. 232.

[10] *Ibid.,* #3120, p. 178.

[11] *The Companion Bible.* London, England: Samuel Bagster & Sons, Limited, 1970, p. 15.

[12] *Op. Cit., Jones' Dictionary of Old Testament Proper Names,* #8493, p. 358.

Chapter 6:

[1] *Webster's New World Dictionary.* Second College Edition, The World Publishing Co., 1970, p. 1122.

[2] *WordPerfect.* Orem, UT: 5.1 WordPerfect Corp. 1990.

[3] *Ibid.*

Chapter 9:

[1] *Ibid.*

[2] *Op. Cit.,* Strong, James, #430, p. 12.

Chapter 10:

[1] *Op. Cit., Jones' Dictionary of Old Testament Proper Names,* #5248, p. 276.

[2] *Op. Cit.,* Strong, James, #7614, p. 111.

³ *Ibid.*, #7652, p. 112.

⁴ *Ibid.*, #'s 1339 & 7651, p. 24.

⁵ *Ibid.*, #3526, p. 50.

Chapter 11:

¹ *Op. Cit., Grolier's Multimedia Encyclopedia.*